CARIBBEAN
COOKING

CARIBBEAN COOKING

Judy Bastyra

HEINEMANN
Kingston

Acknowledgements

I would like to thank the following people for all their help during the writing of this book: Anne Lynch for working so hard at all hours to test the recipes, Mary Tayleur and Simone Sindermann for typing the manuscript, and my many West Indian friends who gave me advice, inspiration and a number of their favorite recipes: Grania de Gannes, Wendy Gregory, Marie Gurly, Caroline Lewis, John Lloyd, Jennifer Mombru, Suzie Montano, Lady Marjorie Pierre, Lady Enid dos Santos and many others too numerous to mention who have entertained me in their homes over the years. Finally I would like to thank my husband Gilbert, who was responsible for introducing me to the delights of the Caribbean.

American consultant: Jenni Fleetwood

House Editor: *Julia Canning*
Editor: *Nicole Foster*
Designer: *Glynis Edwards*
Production: *Richard Churchill*

Photography: *Grant Symon*
Illustrations: *Linda Smith*
Home Economist: *Jane Suthering*
Stylist: *Sue Russell*

First published in Jamaica 1989
by Heinemann Publishers (Caribbean) Ltd.
175 Mountain View Avenue, Kingston 6, Jamaica

ISBN 976-605-079-1

Printed and bound in Portgual

CONTENTS

INTRODUCTION
10

SOUPS
14

APPETIZERS AND SNACKS
22

FISH DISHES
34

MEAT DISHES
50

VEGETABLE DISHES AND RELISHES
70

DESSERTS
98

CAKES, BREADS AND DUMPLINGS
110

DRINKS
118

GLOSSARY AND INDEX
122

INTRODUCTION
A FLAVOR OF THE ISLANDS

I first became interested in Caribbean cooking on my honeymoon thirteen years ago. I arrived in Trinidad with my West Indian husband, eager to drink in all the wonderful sights, sounds and tastes of the tropics. I was not disappointed. Everything was more vivid than anything I'd ever seen before – and the food, a myriad of flavors, exotic, spicy and very, very tasty. Now I invite you to share my experiences of the culinary delights of the Caribbean islands.

Ingredients

As with most cuisines in the world, the best food is rarely found in hotels and restaurants but in the homes of the local people. I was fortunate to meet on my first trip a wonderful cook, Alice, who introduced me to some of the basic techniques and ingredients which are used throughout the islands.

The cuisine of the Caribbean can be described as substantial and spicy. It is based around the wide variety of tropical fruits and vegetables that grow on the islands; guavas, bananas, mangoes, limes, oranges, papaya, pineapple, coconut, okra, plantain, sweet potatoes, yam, cassava, breadfruit and pigeon peas.

Fish plays a dominant role as there is an abundance to be found in the surrounding waters. Chicken, pork and goat are the most popular meats, being easy to rear in the climate.

Seasoning: Seasoning is the very essence of Caribbean cooking, each island having its own special combination of herbs – sive (similar to chives), thyme, scallion, onion, garlic and a little celery is a typical combination. They are all blended together, sometimes with a little water added and kept in a screw-top jar in the refrigerator.

Hot seasoning peppers are very important in all Caribbean cooking. There are many varieties throughout the islands; some can be quite lethal if used without discretion but when used in moderation they add a distinctive flavor. Spices also, such as ginger, nutmeg and cinnamon, are used to season many of the dishes.

Traveling through the islands one soon finds dishes common to many, though each island usually claims the dish solely as its own. For example the Jamaican Stamp and Go (see page 25) can be found in Martinique and Guadeloupe as acrats de morue or in Puerto Rico as bacalaitos.

Another inter-island specialty is Callaloo (Crab and Spinach Soup, see page 14). This thick spicy soup can be found throughout the Caribbean, changing slightly with each island.

There are certain dishes and food, however, that belong solely to one particular island. Salt Fish and Ackee (see page 32) is found only in Jamaica; fried mountain chicken or crapaud – a large edible frog – is a delicacy particular to the island of Dominica and roti is one of the most popular dishes of Trinidad – a flat Indian bread stuffed with curried goat, chicken, shrimp or vegetables, folded and eaten as a filling snack.

History of the Islands

The Amerindians

Two thousand years ago the Arawaks and the Caribs, Amerindian tribes originating from Venezuela and Guyana, settled in the islands of the Caribbean. They both hunted, fished and grew crops. The Arawaks, a gentle people, were better farmers than the warlike Caribs, who were adept at hunting.

They ate similar diets of maize, cassava, sweet potatoes, arrowroot, beans and peppers. They gathered wild fruit and caught wild game.

A favorite dish was pepperpot, a mixed meat and vegetable stew. Pepperpot is now made solely with mixed meats, hot pepper and cassareep – the boiled juice of grated cassava. It is said that some pepperpots are kept going for years, with fresh meat being added to the pot every few days while some are even passed on from generation to generation.

The Europeans

The Spanish: In 1492 Christopher Columbus set sail for the Far East in search of gold and riches for the King and Queen of Spain. When Columbus arrived on Watling Island in the Bahamas in October 1492 he thought he had finally reached the East (or the Indies as it was then known). He stopped briefly on Cuba and then sailed on to Hispaniola (now called Haiti and the Dominican Republic), which was to become the first Caribbean colony of Spain.

In the following years the islands of Cuba, Jamaica and Puerto Rico, which together with Hispaniola make up the Great Antilles, all became Spanish colonies. To the south in the Leeward and Windward islands there was little Spanish penetration, though a small colony of Spaniards did settle in Trinidad.

The gentle Arawaks were soon exploited by the colonists, who put them to work cultivating their crops, digging for gold and using them as slaves. Within 100 years most of the Arawaks were wiped out, by both war and disease.

These early colonists brought with them many of the fruit and vegetables that we now associate with the Caribbean; limes, oranges, mangoes, bananas, breadfruit, tamarind, ginger, coffee, coconut and sugar cane.

Many Spanish dishes still remain in the Caribbean cooking of today: Escovitch (Marinated Cooked Fish, see page 24), bacalaitos or Stamp and Go (Salt Cod Fritters, see page 25) and Cocido de Rinones (Kidney Stew, see page 69).

The British and the French: The British and the French soon challenged the supremacy of Spain in the New World and began to claim many of the Lesser Antilles as their own.

St Christopher, also known as St Kitt, was the first English colony to be founded in the Caribbean by Thomas Warner in 1624. A few years later a French buccaneer, Pierre d'Esnambuc, arrived and the English and French agreed to share the island between them. The English went on to colonize Barbados, Nevis, Montserrat and Antigua. The French spread to Martinique, Guadeloupe, Dominica, St Lucia and Grenada.

Barbados in particular has retained much of the British influence. For example, one of the dishes that is traditionally served at Christmas time in Barbados is called jug-jug. It is made from a purée of pigeon peas, herbs, salted meats and ground millet, and is supposedly a corruption of haggis, which was originally brought to Barbados by Scots in exile there after the Monmouth Rebellion in 1685.

The islands of Guadeloupe and Martinique have remained French. Both are still *départements* of France and as such enjoy a regular supply of French foods, giving the Caribbean cuisine a mixture of European sophistication and creole spice.

The Dutch: The Dutch were better traders than colonists and colonized only a few small islands which they used primarily as trade depots: Curaçao, Aruba, Saba, St Eustatius and St Martin. They have given the Caribbean one of its most interesting dishes – Keshy Yena (Shrimp-filled Edam Cheese, see page 48) – and the orange-flavored liqueur Curaçao.

They were also to have a profound influence on Caribbean history through their brief experience of colonization of the rich Brazilian sugar-cane planting area of Pernambuca. Although the Spanish had grown sugar cane imported from plantations in the Canary Islands, it was the Dutch who brought the ideas and technology from Brazil for planting sugar cane on a large scale and making it by far the most profitable crop to produce. The only problem was that it was labor-intensive. There were not enough Amerindians left to work the plantations, so the importation of African slaves began – over fifteen million being imported into the Americas and the Caribbean between 1518 and 1865.

The Africans

When the slaves arrived they brought with them many plants from Africa which still feature strongly

ATLANTIC OCEAN

The Bahamas

Caicos & Turks Islands

Cuba

G R E A T E R

Cayman Islands

Jamaica

A N T I L L E S

Haiti Dominican Republic

Puerto Rico

Virgin Islands

L E S S E R

Saba St Martin
St Eustatius Antigua
St Kitts Montserrat
Nevis
Guadeloupe

Dominica

Martinique

St Lucia

St Vincent

Grenada

A N T I L L E S

Barbados

CARIBBEAN SEA

Aruba
Curaçao

Tobago

Trinidad

in West Indian cooking – pigeon peas, yam, okra and taro. They were given small rations of salt meat and salt fish and supplemented their diet by growing food. Through their imaginative use of seasoning and spices there evolved a style of cooking characteristic of Caribbean cooking today.

Many of the traditional dishes have survived: Coo Coo (Cornmeal and Okra Pudding, see page 85) and Callaloo (Crab and Spinach Soup, see page 14) are just two examples.

The Indians and the Chinese

By the 1830s when slavery was abolished in many of the islands the system of Indentured Labor was introduced, bringing the East Indians and the Chinese to the Caribbean. They also brought their own culinary expertize with them. Roti, dal puri (puréed split peas), curried goat and Pineapple Spare Ribs (see page 61) have all evolved through their influence.

Creole Cooking

The word "Creole" is synonymous with the Caribbean. It was first used to describe people who were born in the Americas or Caribbeans of pure European descent. Today it is more often applied in the Caribbean to persons of mixed African and European descent. The term Creole food is used to describe many of the Caribbean dishes of mixed African and European influence.

The Cooking of Today

History has now come full circle with Caribbean people living in many countries all over the world. A few years ago very few people outside the tropics had ever tasted a fresh mango, let alone sampled ackee or breadfruit. All these are now available in many of our local street markets and ethnic stores, giving us the opportunity to learn from Caribbean culture and enjoy a flavor of the islands.

SOUPS

It is surprising how enjoyable a bowl of soup can be whether you live in a hot or cold climate. Nothing goes to waste in a Caribbean kitchen and it is the rich homemade stocks which form the basis of their soups that make them so special. Some of the soups such as Pepper Pot Soup (see page 21) are spicy and substantial, while others like Pumpkin Soup (see page 18) or Chicken Consommé with Peppers (see page 21) make a light and appetizing first course.

Crab and Spinach Soup
Callaloo

This delicious thick spicy soup is made from taro leaves, okra, coconut and crab meat. The taro leaves grow on a bush that has an edible root called dasheen and rather confusingly, the leaves are known locally as either "dasheen" leaves or callaloo leaves, after the above dish. However, fresh spinach makes a very good substitute.

Callaloo is found throughout the Caribbean, with each island having its own variation; some have salt pork or bacon which gives a richer stock, while others serve it with the crab claws or the crab meat still in its shell and it is often served as a nourishing meal with the addition of Cornmeal Dumplings (see page 116).

½lb "dasheen" leaves or 1lb fresh spinach
1 tablespoon butter
1 tablespoon oil
1 onion, minced
2 garlic cloves, crushed
¼lb okra, trimmed and sliced
1 fresh chili, seeded and minced
1 sprig fresh thyme
1 teaspoon minced fresh chives
4 cups homemade chicken stock
1¼ cups coconut milk (see page 16)
salt and freshly ground black pepper
½lb crab meat, thawed if frozen
Trinidad Pepper Sauce (see page 95) (optional)

Serves 6

1 Wash the "dasheen" or spinach leaves, drain and finely shred.

2 Heat the butter with the oil in a large saucepan over medium heat, add the onion and garlic and cook for 5 minutes, stirring occasionally, until soft and golden. Add the okra, chili, thyme and chives and cook for a further 5 minutes, stirring constantly.

3 Stir in the "dasheen" or spinach leaves and cook for 3 minutes, turning the leaves to ensure they are evenly cooked. Pour over the stock and coconut milk and season with salt and freshly ground black pepper to taste.

4 Bring to a boil, lower the heat, cover the pan and simmer the soup for 30 minutes.

5 Stir in the crab meat and cook for 5 minutes, until heated through. Taste and adjust the seasoning, adding a little pepper sauce if desired. Serve immediately in warmed soup bowls.

Crab and Spinach Soup

Corn Chowder

Corn Chowder can be made with milk or chicken stock. Served with freshly made popcorn, this filling soup is almost a meal in itself.

1 tablespoon oil
6 bacon slices, diced
1 large Bermuda onion, minced
2 celery stalks, minced
1 green pepper, seeded and diced
2 tomatoes, peeled, seeded and diced
2 potatoes, peeled and diced
1 can (12oz) vacuum-packed whole kernel corn
3 cups milk or chicken stock
1 teaspoon salt
freshly ground black pepper
dash of hot pepper sauce (Tabasco)

For the popcorn
2 tablespoons oil
⅓ cup popcorn
salt

Serves 6

1 Heat the oil in a large saucepan, and sauté the diced bacon over medium heat for 5 minutes until crisp and brown.

2 Using a slotted spoon, transfer the bacon to paper towels to drain.

3 Add the onion to the pan and sauté for 5 minutes, until soft and golden. Stir in the celery, green pepper, tomatoes and potatoes and cook the vegetables for a further 3 minutes.

4 Add the corn and pour over the milk or stock. Season with salt, pepper and a dash of hot pepper sauce. Bring gently to the simmering point and simmer for 15 minutes.

5 Meanwhile make the popcorn: Heat the oil in a large skillet and add the popcorn kernels. Cover the pan and, holding the lid on tightly, shake the pan from time to time as soon as the corn starts popping. When all the popping has stopped remove the lid, discard any imperfect kernels and transfer the popcorn to a serving bowl. Sprinkle over salt to taste. Alternatively, cook the corn in an electric popper, following the manufacturer's directions.

6 To serve, ladle the soup into warmed soup bowls and sprinkle over the crispy bacon. Pass the popcorn separately.

Making Coconut Milk and Cream

To open a coconut: Pierce the eyes of the coconut and drain out the liquid. Place the coconut on a cloth on a firm surface and split it open with a cleaver or hammer. Remove and shred the flesh. Remove the brown skin if the flesh is to be used in a recipe.
To make fresh coconut milk: Purée the flesh and liquid of one fresh coconut with 1 cup boiling water in a blender or food processor, then press through a strainer lined with unbleached muslin, twisting the cloth to extract all the liquid from the flesh (makes about 1½ cups). For a less rich milk, mix the coconut flesh and water in the same way and set aside for 1 hour before straining as above. For a thinner milk, repeat the above process twice, using an additional cup of water.

To make quick coconut milk: Use shredded or flaked coconut in the same way as fresh (6 cups shredded or flaked coconut is equal to 3 fresh coconuts), and substitute hot milk for water for a richer result. Packaged coconut cream can be mixed with water to make varying thicknesses of coconut milk. Canned coconut milk is available from health food stores and specialist markets.
To make coconut cream: Make fresh coconut milk, using half the amount of water, and set aside until the cream rises to the top.

Black-Eyed Pea and Coconut Soup

Black-eyed peas (sometimes called beans) give this thick and spicy soup an interesting nutty flavor. Cowpeas, which are like black-eyed peas but smaller, may also be used. Serve with crusty French bread and a cooling glass of white wine.

1¼ cups dried black-eyed peas
10oz piece smoked ham (preferably on the bone)
1 bay leaf
2 onions, chopped
2 whole cloves
1 teaspoon sugar
1 tablespoon oil
2 tomatoes, peeled and chopped
2½ cups coconut milk (see left)
2 sprigs fresh thyme
1 teaspoon salt
freshly ground black pepper
1 hot seasoning pepper
¼ cup sherry or rum

Serves 6

1 Soak the peas in cold water overnight.

2 Drain and refresh under cold water. Put the peas in a large saucepan with the smoked ham.

3 Pour in enough cold water to cover (about 5 cups), add the bay leaf, half the chopped onion, cloves and sugar and bring to a boil over medium heat. Boil for 10 minutes, skimming off any foam that rises to the surface. Lower the heat, cover the pan and simmer for 45 minutes, or until the peas are cooked and the meat is tender. Remove from the heat and strain the stock into a bowl. Add the peas to the strained stock.

4 Trim the meat from the ham bone, discarding any skin or fat and cut into small dice. Set aside.

5 Heat the oil in a saucepan and sauté the remaining onion for 5 minutes over medium heat, stirring constantly, until soft and golden. Add the tomatoes and cook for 3 minutes, stirring constantly.

6 Pour over the coconut milk and add the reserved peas and stock. Season with thyme, salt, freshly ground black pepper and the seasoning pepper and bring to a boil. Lower the heat, cover and cook for 5 minutes.

7 Remove from the heat and discard the seasoning pepper. Let cool slightly before puréeing in a blender or food processor.

8 Pour the soup into a clean saucepan. Add the reserved ham and sherry or rum and cook gently over low heat for 5 minutes until heated through.

9 Taste and adjust seasoning. Ladle into warmed soup bowls and serve immediately.

Pumpkin Soup

Pumpkin Soup is packed full of vitamins, using the cooking liquor as stock. Pale orange in color, it is found throughout the Caribbean and is often known as Sunshine Soup.

1 pumpkin (about 2 lb), peeled, seeded and cut in 1 inch cubes
salt and freshly ground black pepper
2 tablespoons butter
1 large onion, minced
3 scallions, trimmed and minced
3 tomatoes, peeled and chopped
1 cup coconut milk (see page 16)
¼ teaspoon grated nutmeg
pinch of cayenne
⅔ cup dairy sour cream

Serves 4-6

1 Put the pumpkin in a saucepan, add enough water to cover (about 4 cups) and 1 teaspoon of salt. Bring to a boil. Lower the heat and simmer for 20 minutes. Drain, and reserve the cooking liquor.

2 Melt the butter in a saucepan over medium heat. Add the onion and scallions and sauté, stirring constantly, for 5 minutes until soft and golden.

3 Add the pumpkin, tomatoes, coconut milk, 3 cups of the pumpkin cooking liquor, half the nutmeg, a pinch of cayenne and salt and black pepper to taste. Bring to a boil, lower the heat, cover and simmer for 30 minutes.

4 Remove the pan from the heat, let cool slightly, then purée the soup in two batches in a blender or food processor. Return to the pan and heat for 5 minutes, stirring, until warmed through.

5 Pour the soup into a warmed soup tureen and swirl sour cream on top. Sprinkle with the remaining nutmeg and serve the soup at once.

Tomato and Sweet Potato Soup

Sweet potatoes are one of the more interesting of the starchy vegetables from the Caribbean. Their slight sweetness combined with tomatoes gives a distinctive flavor.

1 tablespoon oil
1 tablespoon butter
2 onions, minced
½ lb sweet potatoes, peeled and diced
1 lb tomatoes, peeled and finely chopped
juice and grated rind of 1 large orange
4 cups chicken stock
1 teaspoon oregano
1 teaspoon salt
freshly ground black pepper

For garnish
1 orange, thinly sliced
1 tomato, thinly sliced

Serves 6

1 Heat the oil and butter together in a saucepan over medium heat. Add the onions and cook for 5 minutes, or until soft and golden.

2 Add the sweet potatoes, tomatoes, orange juice and rind, chicken stock, oregano, salt and pepper and bring to a boil. Lower the heat, cover the pan and simmer the soup for 20 minutes.

3 Remove the pan from the heat and let cool slightly. Purée half the soup at a time in a blender or food processor.

4 Return to the pan and heat for 5 minutes until warmed through.

5 To serve, ladle into warmed soup bowls and garnish with a slice of orange and a slice of tomato.

Pumpkin Soup

Fish and Coconut Soup
Sopito

Fish and Coconut Soup is better known as Sopito in the Dutch islands of Curaçao and Aruba. The tasty combination of coconut milk, fish, salt meat, hot seasoning pepper and spices gives this delicious soup its unusual flavor. It is sometimes made with cream, making it a much richer dish.

2 onions
1 garlic clove
2 bay leaves
1 celery stalk, chopped
1 leek, chopped
1 teaspoon whole peppercorns
1 tablespoon minced fresh basil
1 teaspoon cumin seeds
salt
1 lb whole fish, red snapper, sea bass, pollock or mullet, cleaned and scaled
¼ lb salt beef, diced
2 whole cloves
1 hot seasoning pepper
1 ¼ cups coconut milk, made with fresh coconut (see page 16)
3 tablespoons cornmeal
1 ½ cups shrimp, in shells
1 tablespoon minced fresh basil, for garnish

Serves 6

1 Slice one of the onions and put it in a saucepan with the garlic, bay leaves, celery, leek, peppercorns, 1 tablespoon basil, cumin and 1 teaspoon of salt. Pour over 5 cups cold water and bring to a boil over medium heat. Lower the heat, cover the pan and simmer for 15 minutes.

2 Add the fish and cook for 10-15 minutes, until the fish flakes easily when tested with a fork.

3 Remove the pan from the heat and strain the stock into a clean pan. Reserve the fish.

4 Mince the remaining onion and add this to the fish stock along with the diced beef, cloves, seasoning pepper and coconut milk.

5 Bring to a boil over medium heat. Lower the heat, cover and simmer for 45 minutes, or until the beef is tender. Remove the seasoning pepper after 15 minutes and discard.

6 Sprinkle over the cornmeal and cook for 2 minutes, stirring constantly.

7 Skin and bone the fish and cut it in 1 inch pieces. Add the fish and shrimp to the soup and cook over low heat for 5 minutes to heat through.

8 To serve, ladle into warmed soup bowls and sprinkle over the chopped basil to garnish.

Pepper Pot Soup

A filling and spicy soup made with vegetables, meat and shrimp which is found on several of the Caribbean islands. It is often confused with another well-known Caribbean dish called "Pepperpot" made from mixed meat, seasonings and cassareep. Like Pepperpot, this soup improves with age, so make it the day before it is to be served.

1 lb beef shank, cut in ½ inch cubes
½ lb salt beef, cut in ½ inch cubes
1 lb fresh spinach, trimmed
salt and freshly ground black pepper
2 onions, minced
2 garlic cloves, crushed
1 teaspoon dried thyme
1 hot seasoning pepper
1 lb tannias, peeled and cut in 1 inch cubes
1 ½ cups uncooked (green) shrimp, in shells
5 cups beef stock
2 tablespoons butter
¼ lb okra, trimmed and finely sliced

Serves 6-8

1 Put the beef and salt beef into a large saucepan. Pour over enough cold water to cover (about 10 cups) and bring to a boil. Lower the heat and simmer for 1½ hours.

2 Put the spinach in another pan and cover with cold water. Add 1 teaspoon of salt and bring to a boil over medium heat. Cook for 10 minutes, then drain. Transfer to a blender or food processor and work for 30 seconds until the spinach forms a smooth purée.

3 Add the spinach purée to the meat in the saucepan, along with the onions, garlic, thyme, seasoning pepper, tannias and shrimp, and season to taste with salt and black pepper. Pour over the stock and bring to a boil over medium heat. Lower the heat and simmer for 20 minutes, or until the meat and tannias are tender.

4 Melt the butter in a small skillet, add the okra and sauté over medium heat, stirring constantly for 5 minutes or until lightly browned. Add to the soup and cook for 5 minutes.

5 Remove the seasoning pepper, transfer to a warmed soup tureen and serve immediately.

Chicken Consommé with Peppers

This delicate consommé, flavored with sweet peppers and a dash of sherry or Pepper Wine (see page 95), makes the perfect beginning to any Caribbean meal.

2 scallions, trimmed and finely sliced
1 green pepper, seeded and finely sliced
1 sweet red pepper, seeded and finely sliced
dry sherry or Pepper Wine (see page 95), to serve

For the stock
3 ½ lb broiler-fryer
1 large onion, chopped
2 carrots, chopped
1 celery stalk, chopped
½ sweet red pepper, seeded and chopped
1 tomato, chopped
1 small turnip, chopped
1 teaspoon salt
1 teaspoon sugar
1 teaspoon whole black peppercorns

Serves 8

1 First make the stock: Wash the chicken, then place it in a large saucepan. Add the onion, carrots, celery, sweet red pepper, tomato, turnip, salt, sugar and peppercorns. Pour over enough cold water to cover (about 12½ cups) and bring to a boil over medium heat. Boil for 10 minutes, skimming off any foam that rises to the surface.

2 Lower the heat, cover the pan and simmer for 3 hours. Drain the stock into a bowl and let stand until cool, then cover the bowl with plastic wrap and refrigerate overnight.

3 Remove the fat from the surface of the stock, then strain the stock into a saucepan.

4 Heat the stock until just simmering, then add the scallions, green and sweet red peppers. Cook the soup for 4 minutes.

5 To serve, ladle into warmed soup bowls and add a dash of sherry or pepper wine to each bowl.

APPETIZERS AND SNACKS

My favorite dishes in the Caribbean have always been the Appetizers and Snacks. Many of the dishes in the snack section are eaten as light meals by themselves at varying times of the day. For example Salt Cod Salad (Buljol, see page 24) and Cornmeal and Meat Packages (Pastelles, see page 30) can be eaten for breakfast, lunch or supper.

Fish Mousse

This delicate creamy Fish Mousse from Martinique makes an impressive appetizer for a dinner party. Serve the mousse with hot Melba toast and a bottle of cold Chablis.

In Martinique red snapper would be used for this dish, but any firm-fleshed white fish can be used as a substitute.

1 teaspoon oil
¾lb white fish fillets, snapper, haddock or pollock
1 onion, sliced
1 bay leaf
6 whole peppercorns
1 teaspoon salt
1 package (8oz) cream cheese, softened
6 tablespoons mayonnaise
1 tablespoon minced onion
⅔ cup shelled cooked shrimp, chopped
1 tablespoon minced fresh parsley
1 tablespoon minced fresh chives
⅛ teaspoon cayenne
pinch of grated nutmeg
1 tablespoon unflavored gelatin
juice of 2 limes

For garnish
1 bunch watercress, trimmed
1 lime, sliced

Serves 8

1 Using the teaspoon of oil lightly grease a 5-cup fish-shaped or plain mold.

2 Place the fish in a saucepan and cover with cold water. Add the sliced onion, bay leaf, peppercorns and salt. Bring to a boil over a medium heat. Lower the heat, cover the pan and simmer for 10 minutes, or until the fish flakes easily when tested with a fork.

3 Drain the fish, remove any bones and discard the seasonings. Put the fish in a blender or food processor with the cream cheese, mayonnaise and minced onion and work for 30 seconds to a smooth purée.

4 Add the shrimp, parsley, chives, cayenne and nutmeg and process for 15 seconds.

5 Sprinkle the gelatin over the lime juice in a heatproof bowl. Let soak for 5 minutes, then stand the bowl in a pan of gently simmering water for 1-2 minutes until the gelatin has completely dissolved, stirring occasionally. Pour the gelatin into the fish mixture. Work for 10 seconds until thoroughly combined. Pour the mixture into the prepared mold, cover with plastic wrap and refrigerate for 2 hours or until set.

6 To serve, line a serving platter with watercress, then dip the bottom of the mold into hot water for a few seconds. Run a knife around inside edge of mold then invert the mousse on the platter, giving a few firm shakes. Decorate with lime slices.

Fish Mousse (left) and Salt Cod Salad

Marinated Cooked Fish
Escovitch

Escovitch comes from the Spanish word "escabeche", which is a popular cooking method of pickling cooked fish in vinegar.

2¼lb fish fillets, cod, red snapper,
mackerel, pompano or salmon
juice of 2 limes
1 onion, minced
1 garlic clove, crushed
1 teaspoon salt
freshly ground black pepper
⅓ cup olive oil

For the sauce
2 tablespoons oil
2 onions, finely sliced
2 garlic cloves, crushed
1 sweet red pepper, seeded and finely sliced
1 green pepper, seeded and finely sliced
1 inch piece of fresh gingerroot, pared and minced
pinch of ground mace
1 tablespoon black peppercorns
2 bay leaves
1 teaspoon salt
¾ cup white wine vinegar

Serves 4-6

1 Flavor the fish with the lime juice, onion, garlic, salt and pepper, cover and marinate for 2 hours.

2 Make the sauce: Heat the oil in a saucepan, add the onions and sauté gently over medium heat for 5 minutes, stirring constantly. Add the garlic, sweet red and green peppers and cook for 3 minutes.

3 Add the remaining ingredients with ½ cup water. Bring to a boil, then lower the heat and simmer for 10 minutes. Remove from the heat.

4 Drain the fish and discard the flavoring ingredients. Pat dry with paper towels. Heat half the oil in a skillet and cook half the fish for 6-8 minutes, or until lightly browned, turning once. Transfer to a shallow serving dish. Repeat with remaining oil and fish.

5 Pour sauce over fish and serve hot or cold.

Salt Cod Salad
Buljol

This spicy salad is a great favorite for Sunday brunch in Trinidad. It is also delicious as an appetizer served on little crackers, to eat with drinks.

This dish should be made the day before you wish to eat it.

½lb salt cod, soaked overnight and drained
juice of 1 lime
1 large Bermuda onion, minced
1 green pepper, seeded and minced
3 tomatoes, chopped
3-4 tablespoons olive oil
2 hard-cooked eggs, finely chopped
2 tablespoons minced fresh parsley
freshly ground black pepper

Serves 6

1 Put the fish in a saucepan, cover with cold water and bring to a boil over medium heat. Lower the heat and simmer for 1 minute. Off heat, drain and refresh under cold water.

2 When just cool enough to handle, remove and discard the skin and bones and shred the fish. Place the shredded fish in a serving bowl.

3 Add the lime juice, onion, green pepper and tomatoes to the warm fish and mix well.

4 Add 3 tablespoons of the oil and, if the salad is a little dry, add the remaining oil. It should be lightly coated with the oil.

5 Stir in the eggs and parsley and black pepper to taste. When completely cool, cover with plastic wrap and refrigerate for at least 4 hours or overnight. Remove from the refrigerator 1 hour before serving.

Trinidad Fried Shark

Salt Cod Fritters
Stamp and Go

One of the many treats of spending a hot Sunday at Maraccas Beach is having an ice cold beer or two with your tasty beach snack of Shark and Bake.

This fearsome animal tastes quite delicious when highly seasoned and fried, then served in the bun-like Bake (see page 117). The brave eat it with generous helpings of Trinidad Pepper Sauce (see page 95), followed by more cool beer to put out the fire. The texture of shark is often compared to that of veal.

2¼lb shark, skinned and cut in 2 inch cubes
¼ cup all-purpose flour
1 teaspoon dried thyme
1 teaspoon salt
freshly ground black pepper
oil, for deep-frying

For the marinade
juice of 2 limes
1 onion, minced
2 garlic cloves, crushed
1 fresh chili, seeded and minced
1 tablespoon dried thyme
1 teaspoon salt

Serves 4-6

1 Make the marinade: Mix the lime juice, onion, garlic, chili, thyme, salt and pepper together.

2 Place the shark cubes in a large mixing bowl, pour on the marinade and mix well, ensuring that all the cubes are coated with the mixture.

3 Cover and place in the refrigerator for at least 2 hours or overnight.

4 Remove the shark from the marinade and pat dry with paper towels.

5 Season the flour with the thyme, salt and pepper and sprinkle onto a plate. Roll each cube in the flour.

6 Heat about 2 inches of oil in a deep skillet over medium heat. When hot, add a few shark cubes at a time and cook for 5-7 minutes. Remove with a slotted spoon and drain on paper towels. Keep warm in a low oven while cooking the remaining shark.

Salt Cod Fritters are to be found throughout the Caribbean, with each island having its own variation.

This recipe is for the Jamaican Stamp and Go – a name which apparently comes from an old nautical term. There are many other local names in the other islands for these fritters, Bacalaitos, Acrat de Morue or Marinades, John Staggerback or Poor Man's Fritters, to name but a few.

½lb salt cod
1 cup all-purpose flour
1 teaspoon baking powder
½ teaspoon salt
1 egg, lightly beaten
¾ cup milk
1 tablespoon melted butter
1 onion, minced
1 fresh red chili, seeded and minced
oil, for deep-frying

Makes 24

1 Soak the salt cod in water overnight. Drain, rinse under cold water, then place in a saucepan and cover with cold water.

2 Place the pan over medium heat and bring to a boil. Reduce the heat, cover the pan and simmer for 10 minutes. Drain, rinse under cold water and, when cool enough to handle, remove and discard the skin and bones and flake the fish. Set aside.

3 Mix the flour, baking powder and salt together in a bowl. Make a well in the center and pour in the egg, milk and melted butter. Mix together with a wooden spoon to a smooth batter, adding a little more milk if necessary. Stir in the onion, chili and flaked fish and mix well.

4 Heat about ½ inch of oil in a large deep skillet until hot but not smoking. Drop tablespoons of the mixture into the oil, a few at a time, spaced well apart. Cook for 3-4 minutes, turning once, or until golden brown.

5 Remove with a slotted spoon and drain on paper towels. Keep warm in a low oven while cooking the remaining fritters. Serve hot.

Hearts of Palm Salad

A sophisticated appetizer from Martinique, this salad is served on individual plates, arranged in the shape of a palm tree. Hearts of palm come from a wide variety of palms. The heart, which is the terminal bud of the palm, is edible and has a firm texture with a rather mild flavor.

Fresh hearts of palm are generally boiled until tender then served either hot with a sauce as a vegetable dish, or cold in a salad.

1 can (14oz) hearts of palm, drained
2 firm ripe avocados
2 firm ripe mangoes, peeled and thinly sliced
juice of ½ lime
¼ head iceberg lettuce, thinly shredded

For the dressing
1 teaspoon dry mustard
1 teaspoon sugar
1 tablespoon mango chutney
2 tablespoons fresh lime juice
⅓ cup olive oil
salt and freshly ground black pepper

Serves 6

1 Make the dressing: Mix the mustard and sugar together in a mixing bowl. Add the chutney and lime juice then, using a balloon whip, gradually beat in the olive oil. Season with salt and pepper to taste, and pour through a strainer into a bowl, to remove any large pieces of mango.

2 Cut 6 large hearts of palm into approximately 1 inch slices and re-form them individually on serving plates to represent palm "trunks". Chop the remaining smaller palm hearts into thinner slices – these will be the "coconuts" – and set aside.

3 Peel and thinly slice the avocados. Arrange alternate slices of mango and avocado at the top of each palm heart "trunk" to make the palm "leaves" and add the remaining sliced palm hearts for the "coconuts". Pour the lime juice over the avocado slices to prevent them from discoloring.

4 Sprinkle a little shredded lettuce along the bottom of each plate for the "grass" and serve with the dressing passed separately.

Shrimp and Watermelon Cocktail

Spicy, sweet and cool, this Shrimp and Watermelon Cocktail characterizes the balance of flavors in West Indian cooking.

Serve this impressive appetizer in tall glasses with thinly sliced brown bread and butter.

1 lb watermelon
2 cups shelled cooked baby shrimp
1 tablespoon fresh lime juice
1 tablespoon gin
¼ head lettuce, finely shredded
1 lime, sliced, for garnish

For the dressing
3 tablespoons mayonnaise
3 tablespoons ketchup
1 teaspoon Worcestershire sauce
1 tablespoon minced onion
1 teaspoon paprika
½ teaspoon salt
½ teaspoon white pepper
dash of hot pepper sauce (Tabasco)

Serves 6

1 Remove the seeds from the watermelon and scoop the flesh into balls using a melon baller.

2 Reserve 18 shrimp and 18 melon balls to use for the garnish.

3 Put the remaining shrimp in a bowl and pour over the lime juice and gin. Set aside.

4 Make the dressing: Mix the mayonnaise, ketchup, Worcestershire, onion, paprika, salt, pepper and hot pepper sauce in a large mixing bowl.

5 Tip the shrimp with their liquid into the dressing and add the melon balls. Mix well to ensure the shrimp and melon are coated with the dressing.

6 Put the shredded lettuce into the bottom of 6 tall glasses. Spoon the shrimp and melon mixture into the glasses. Garnish with the reserved melon balls and shrimp and the lime slices and serve immediately.

Hearts of Palm Salad

Hot Orange and Grapefruit Baskets

A great way to start any Caribbean meal – juicy citrus fruits with a good shot of rum.

These attractive grapefruit baskets are filled with a mixture of grapefruit and orange sections that have been tossed in rum, then sprinkled with dark brown sugar and baked under the broiler until the sugar is bubbling up. Many other citrus fruits may be used for this recipe including limes, tangerines, tangelos, uglis and shaddocks.

2 grapefruit
4 oranges
2-3 tablespoons rum
4 tablespoons dark brown sugar
dash of Angostura bitters

Serves 4

1 Using a small, sharp knife, cut each grapefruit in half using a zig-zag line. Pull the fruit apart and cut the flesh from inside with a grapefruit knife, removing all the pith and leaving a clean grapefruit skin basket. Cut a paper-thin slice from the bottom of each basket to enable it to stand firmly.

2 Cut the pith away from the grapefruit sections and cut the flesh up in chunks. Place the sections in a mixing bowl.

3 Peel and section each orange in the following way: Using a very sharp knife cut off the two ends of each orange. Stand the orange on one end and cut off the skin in a downward motion, taking the pith with the skin. Cut each orange section from between the pithy membranes. Add the orange sections to the grapefruit chunks in the bowl. Pour over the rum and mix well.

4 Spoon the mixture into the grapefruit baskets, decorating the top of each basket with 3 of the orange sections.

5 Preheat the broiler to high.

6 Sprinkle a tablespoon of the sugar over each grapefruit. Place the grapefruit in a broiler pan and broil for 5 minutes, until the fruit is heated through and the sugar is bubbling.

7 Arrange on individual plates, add a dash of Angostura bitters to each portion and serve the grapefruit baskets immediately.

Plantain Chips

Plantain Chips are crunchy, with a mild banana flavor. They can be kept for several weeks in a screw-top jar and eaten as a snack on their own or as the perfect accompaniment to a dip. Plantain Crisps are a must at any West Indian cocktail party.

4 green plantains
oil, for deep-frying
salt

1 Peel the plantains and cut in thin slices.

2 Heat the oil in a deep skillet.

3 When the oil is hot, add the plantain slices, a few at a time, and cook for 2-3 minutes until crisp and golden. Remove them with a slotted spoon and drain on paper towels.

4 Sprinkle over the salt to taste. Serve when cool.

Soused Pigs' Feet
Souse

Soused Pigs' Feet, or Souse as it is sometimes called is traditionally served with black pudding for an informal Sunday brunch. It is often made with "hog features" – pig's head. For a more meaty dish, pork chops may also be added.

4 meaty pigs' feet

For the brine
juice of 12 limes
1-2 tablespoons salt
2 onions, chopped
2 fresh chilies, seeded and minced

For garnish
1 cucumber, pared and sliced
watercress sprigs

Serves 4

1 Put the pigs' feet in a metal colander, then pour over boiling water to scald them. Rinse under cold water and scrape clean with a knife.

2 Put the feet into a large saucepan, cover with cold water, then bring to a boil over medium heat. Lower the heat, cover the pan and simmer the feet for 1½ hours until tender.

3 Drain the feet, then refresh under cold water. When just cool enough to handle, split down the middle, then cut in bite-size pieces and place in a large bowl.

4 Make the brine: Mix the lime juice, salt, onions and chilies together in a bowl, then pour over the warm pigs' feet. Add enough cold water to cover the feet. Cover the bowl with plastic wrap and refrigerate overnight.

5 To serve, remove the feet from the brine and arrange in a serving dish. Garnish with the cucumber slices and watercress.

Cornmeal and Meat Packages
Pastelles

Originally from South America, these banana leaf packages of cornmeal and meat are a national favorite in Trinidad. They make a perfect snack at any time of the day, and are even eaten for breakfast with Hot Pepper Sauce (see page 95).

Making pastelles can be a great way to spend an afternoon, with a group of family or friends forming a production line – one person preparing the banana leaves, another rolling the cornmeal balls, another adding the meat and yet another folding the packages. They are generally made in great quantities just before Christmas but are also eaten throughout the year.

Banana leaves are available from Oriental supermarkets. They are sold either tied in bundles of 5 leaves or in plastic packs of 2-3 leaves.

3 cups coarse cornmeal
2 tablespoons diced shortening
⅓ cup oil
2 teaspoons salt
3-4 banana leaves

For the filling
2 tablespoons oil
1 large onion, minced
1 garlic clove, crushed
1 fresh chili, seeded and minced
½lb stew pork, ground or finely chopped
½lb stew beef, ground or finely chopped
1 teaspoon minced fresh thyme
1 tablespoon minced fresh chives
1 teaspoon minced fresh basil
2 tomatoes, peeled and chopped
½ sweet red pepper, seeded and minced
1 tablespoon Worcestershire sauce
4 tablespoons capers, rinsed and chopped
4 tablespoons raisins
15 olives, chopped
salt and freshly ground black pepper
¾ cup beef stock

Makes 18

1 Make the filling: Heat the oil in a skillet and sauté the onion gently for 5 minutes, or until soft. Stir in the garlic and chili and cook for 3 minutes.

2 Add the pork, beef, thyme, chives and basil and cook for 10-15 minutes, stirring constantly, until the meat is lightly browned.

3 Stir in the tomatoes, pepper, Worcestershire, half the capers, raisins and olives and season. Pour over the stock and bring to a boil. Lower the heat and simmer, uncovered, for 45 minutes, stirring occasionally. Adjust seasoning, then let cool.

4 Put the cornmeal into a large mixing bowl, add the shortening, 2 tablespoons oil and the salt. Pour over 2¾ cups boiling water and mix well to a smooth dough. Form the cornmeal into 18 balls.

5 Cut the banana leaves into thirty-six 8 × 10 inch rectangles. Place in a bowl, then pour over boiling water. Drain, then refresh under cold water. Pat dry.

6 Rub a leaf rectangle with a little of the remaining oil. Place a ball of cornmeal in the center and gently pat down. Wet one of the leaf rectangles and place over the cornmeal. Using a rolling pin, roll the cornmeal out to form a circle about ¼ inch thick, then peel off the top leaf rectangle. Spread 2 tablespoons of the meat filling over the cornmeal and sprinkle over a little of the remaining capers, raisins and olives.

7 Enclose the meat filling with cornmeal by folding half the leaf rectangle over, bringing the cornmeal with it. Flatten leaf rectangle, then repeat with other half of leaf rectangle so that the cornmeal completely encloses the meat. Then fold up the leaf rectangle to make a package. Place the package folded side down on another leaf rectangle, on the opposite grain, and fold to enclose the package, securing with string.

8 Repeat, to make 17 more pastelles. Place in a pan of boiling salted water and simmer for 1½ hours.

9 Drain the pastelles well, then remove the string or foil. Transfer to a large platter and serve.

Cornmeal and Meat Packages

Salt Fish and Ackee

One of the most popular dishes of Jamaica, this can be served as an appetizer or as a main course, with fried plantain and Rice 'n' Peas (see page 80).

Ackees are the fruit of a West African tree (*Blighia sapida*), generally believed to have been named after Captain Bligh. The tree has pear-shaped pods which, when ripe, split open bearing three shiny black seeds each surrounded by a cream-colored aril, which is the edible part. The aril has a delicate flavor and is often compared to "brains" in appearance when uncooked and "scrambled eggs" when cooked. The fruit must be eaten only when just ripe, as both unripe and overripe ackee can be poisonous.

½lb salt cod
2 tablespoons butter
¼ cup olive oil
2 bacon slices, diced
4 scallions, trimmed and minced
1 onion, finely sliced
½ teaspoon dried thyme
2 fresh chilies, seeded and finely sliced
1 green pepper, seeded and finely sliced
2 tomatoes, peeled and chopped
1 can (12oz) ackees, drained
salt and freshly ground black pepper
parsley sprigs, for garnish

Serves 4

1 Put the fish in a saucepan and cover with water. Bring to a boil and cook for 10 minutes. Drain the fish, then rinse under cold water. When cool enough to handle, remove and discard the skin and bones and flake the fish. Set aside.

2 Heat the butter with the oil in a skillet over medium heat. Add the bacon and cook for 5 minutes until quite crisp. Remove with a slotted spoon and drain on paper towels.

3 Sauté the scallions, onion, thyme, chilies and green pepper together in the skillet for 5 minutes, stirring constantly. Add the tomatoes and cook for a further 5 minutes.

4 Stir in the salt cod, ackees and bacon and cook for 2-3 minutes, until heated through.

5 Serve on a warmed dish, garnished with parsley.

Avocado Dip

This hot and spicy dip is a delicious appetizer to pass around with drinks. Serve with Plantain Chips (see page 29) or crudités.

2 ripe avocados
1 tablespoon fresh lime juice
1 garlic clove, crushed
1 tablespoon minced onion
2 packages (3oz size) cream cheese, softened
3 tablespoons coconut milk (see page 16)
⅛ teaspoon ground pimiento
dash of hot pepper sauce (Tabasco)
1 teaspoon ground coriander
salt and freshly ground black pepper
fresh cilantro leaves or parsley, for garnish

Serves 6-8

1 Peel the avocados and mash the pulp with a fork or purée in a blender or food processor until smooth and creamy. Add the lime juice, garlic and onion.

2 Stir in the cream cheese, coconut milk, pimiento, hot pepper sauce and ground coriander. Mix well and season to taste with salt and pepper.

3 Spoon the dip into a serving dish, garnish with the cilantro leaves or parsley and serve immediately. If you wish to make the dip a few hours before serving, keep one of the avocado seeds and immerse it in the dip. Cover closely with plastic wrap and refrigerate. This will prevent the avocado from discoloring unattractively.

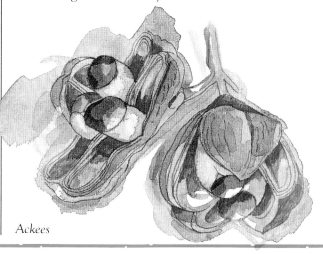

Ackees

Jamaican Beef Patties

One of the most popular lunchtime snacks in Jamaica, these patties are a great alternative to the American hamburger or the English sandwich.

They were brought to Jamaica from Haiti with the immigrants who settled there in the 18th century. They are best eaten freshly baked as they tend to dry out if kept for any length of time. Commercially prepared curry powder may be used as an alternative to the different spices used to flavor the meat.

For the pastry
4 cups all-purpose flour
2 teaspoons turmeric
1 teaspoon salt
1 cup shortening

For the filling
2 tablespoons oil
1 onion, minced
2 scallions, trimmed and minced
1-2 garlic cloves, crushed
2 fresh chilies, seeded and minced
¾lb ground beef
4 tomatoes, peeled and chopped
¼ teaspoon turmeric
¼ teaspoon ground cumin
¼ teaspoon ground coriander
¼ teaspoon ground fenugreek
¼ teaspoon ground ginger
⅛ teaspoon ground cinnamon
⅛ teaspoon ground cardamom
salt and freshly ground black pepper
2 egg yolks, beaten

Makes 12

1 Make the pastry: Sift the flour, turmeric and salt into a bowl. Cut in the shortening and rub in until the mixture resembles coarse meal. Add 3 tablespoons of ice water to form a firm dough. Cover the dough with plastic wrap and refrigerate for 2 hours or longer.

2 Meanwhile, prepare the filling: Heat the oil in a skillet, add the onion and sauté over medium heat for 5 minutes, until soft and golden. Stir in the scallions, garlic and chilies and cook for 3 minutes.

3 Add the beef and cook, stirring frequently, for 10 minutes. Stir in the tomatoes, turmeric, cumin, coriander, fenugreek, ginger, cinnamon and cardamom and season to taste with salt and freshly ground pepper.

4 Pour in ½ cup water, reduce the heat to low and cook for 20 minutes, stirring frequently. Set aside to cool.

5 Preheat the oven to 400°F.

6 Roll out the pastry and cut into 12 rounds, approximately 7 inches in diameter, using a saucer as a guide.

7 Put 2 tablespoons of the filling on one side of each pastry round then fold over to form a crescent. Crimp the edges with a fork to seal them. Arrange on an ungreased baking sheet and brush the top of each patty with a little beaten egg yolk.

8 Bake in the center of the oven for 25-30 minutes until golden brown.

9 Transfer to a large serving platter and serve the beef patties at once.

FISH DISHES

One of the most delightful experiences in the Caribbean is to get up early in the morning to meet the local fishing boats and choose your fish for the day. The choice is quite dazzling: Silver-winged flying fish, rosy red snapper, lobsters, shrimp and many many more. Although the Caribbean waters abound with fresh fish, salt cod is still used a great deal. Dating from the days of slavery, its distinctive flavor is essential to many traditional dishes.

Poached Fish with Avocado Sauce

This elegant dish can be served either hot or cold. Garnish the fish with the avocado slices just before serving to avoid discoloration.

1 onion, sliced
1 celery stalk, sliced
1 carrot, sliced
1 lime, sliced
½ teaspoon whole black peppercorns
1 bay leaf
1 tablespoon minced fresh parsley
1 sprig fresh thyme
1¼ cups dry white wine
2 whole fish, each weighing 3lb, porgy, rockfish
or sea bass, cleaned

For the sauce
2 firm ripe avocados
2 tablespoons fresh lime juice
2 tablespoons olive oil
1 tablespoon minced onion
2 garlic cloves, crushed
¼ teaspoon dried oregano
1 teaspoon salt
freshly ground black pepper

For garnish
2 stuffed olives, sliced
2 small firm ripe avocados
1 tablespoon fresh lime juice
fresh cilantro leaves

Serves 8

1 Put the onion, celery, carrot, lime, peppercorns, bay leaf, parsley, thyme and wine into a fish kettle. Pour over 10 cups of water and bring to a boil. Lower the heat, cover with the lid and simmer for 20 minutes.

2 Place the fish on the poaching tray and gently lower them into the liquor. If necessary add a little more water to cover the fish and bring back to a boil. Lower the heat, cover and simmer for 5 minutes. Switch off the heat and let the fish cool in the liquor for 1 hour.

3 Lift out the tray and carefully skin one side of each fish, leaving the skin on the head. Carefully transfer each fish to a serving platter, skinned side down, and skin the other half.

4 Make the sauce: Peel and chop the avocados. Put them with the lime juice, olive oil, onion, garlic, oregano, salt and pepper into a blender or food processor and work for 30 seconds or until the mixture forms a smooth purée.

5 Spread the avocado purée over the skinned part of the fish, but not the heads and tails. Cover each eye with olive slices. Peel, quarter and thinly slice the avocados. Put them in a bowl, pour over the lime juice and mix gently. Garnish the fish with the sliced avocado to form "scales", decorate with cilantro leaves and serve immediately.

Poached Fish with Avocado Sauce

Frizzled Salt Cod

This is a rather exotic way of serving scrambled eggs. Salt cod can be bought from many delicatessens either in a whole piece or filleted and wrapped in plastic. Shredded salt cod is also sold in 2oz packages.

½lb salt cod, soaked overnight and drained
3 bacon slices, minced
¼lb fresh spinach, washed, dried and minced
2 tablespoons butter
2 tablespoons oil
1 onion, minced
3 scallions, trimmed and minced
2 tomatoes, minced
½ sweet red pepper, seeded and minced
½ teaspoon dried basil
salt and freshly ground black pepper
2 eggs, beaten
1 tablespoon minced fresh chives, for garnish

Serves 4

1 Put the salt cod in a saucepan. Pour over enough cold water to cover and bring to a boil over medium heat. Lower the heat and simmer for 5 minutes. Drain and refresh under cold water. When cool enough to handle, remove and discard the skin and bones.

2 Put the fish in a blender or food processor and process for 30 seconds. Transfer to a bowl.

3 Add the bacon and spinach to the salt cod in the bowl and mix well.

4 Melt the butter in the oil in a heavy-bottomed skillet over medium heat. Add the onion and sauté, stirring constantly for 5 minutes, until soft and golden.

5 Stir in the fish mixture, scallions, tomatoes, sweet red pepper and basil. Add salt and pepper to taste and cook over medium to high heat for 5 minutes, stirring frequently.

6 Pour over the beaten eggs and cook, stirring constantly for 2 minutes until the eggs are cooked.

7 Transfer to a warmed serving dish, sprinkle over the chives and serve immediately.

Fish with Cilantro and Coconut

Fish with Cilantro and Coconut reflects the South American influence on the cooking of the Caribbean. Serve with Creole Rice (see page 81) and Avocado and Pink Grapefruit Salad (see page 90). Cilantro, also known as coriander was brought originally from southern Europe.

1½lb cod fillets, skinned
juice of 1 lime
salt and freshly ground black pepper
2 Bermuda onions, thinly sliced
2 tablespoons olive oil
4 scallions, trimmed and chopped
2 garlic cloves, crushed
1 fresh chili, seeded and minced
1 can (16oz) tomatoes, drained and chopped
3 tablespoons minced fresh parsley
5 tablespoons minced fresh cilantro
2½ cups coconut milk (see page 16)
cilantro sprigs, for garnish

Serves 6

1 Put the fish fillets in a glass or china dish. Pour over the lime juice. Add 1 teaspoon of salt and half the sliced onions. Mix the ingredients together and set aside for 30 minutes.

2 Heat the oil in a large heavy-bottomed skillet, add the remaining onion and sauté for 5 minutes over medium heat. Add the scallions, garlic and chili and cook for 2 minutes, stirring constantly.

3 Add the tomatoes and cook for a further 5 minutes.

4 Lay the fish fillets in the pan and spoon over the tomato sauce. Sprinkle over the parsley and cilantro. Season to taste with salt and black pepper. Pour over the coconut milk, and bring to a boil. Lower heat, cover pan and simmer for 15 minutes.

5 Taste and adjust the seasoning. Transfer to a warmed serving platter and garnish with cilantro sprigs. Serve immediately.

Martinique Poached Fish
Court Bouillon de Poisson

Martinique Poached Fish is an adaptation of one of the most characteristic dishes of the French islands, Court Bouillon de Poisson. The term "Court Bouillon" does not refer to the cooking liquor used for poaching as in French cooking, but in this case is used to mean a fish cooked in a special sauce. In Martinique or Guadaloupe Court Bouillon de Poisson would be finished with the addition of raw garlic and freshly-squeezed lime juice. Serve with Creole Rice (see page 81), fried ripe plantain and Baked Chayotes au Gratin (see page 73).

2¼lb whole fish, gray mullet or mackerel, cleaned, scaled
and cut in 1 inch slices
1 hot seasoning pepper, seeded and minced
2 garlic cloves, crushed
2 tablespoons minced fresh chives
¼ cup fresh lime juice
1 teaspoon salt
2 tablespoons minced fresh chives, for garnish

For the sauce
2 tablespoons butter
2 tablespoons olive oil
6 scallions, trimmed and minced
6 tomatoes, peeled and chopped
2 tablespoons minced fresh parsley
2 tablespoons minced fresh chives
salt and freshly ground black pepper
¼ cup fresh lime juice
¾ cup dry white wine
4 garlic cloves, crushed

Serves 4-6

1 Put the fish in a large glass or china dish; pour in enough cold water to cover. Add the seasoning pepper, garlic cloves, chives, lime juice and salt and set aside to marinate for 1 hour.

2 Make the sauce: Heat the butter and oil together in a large heavy-bottomed skillet. Add the scallions and cook for 3 minutes. Add the tomatoes, parsley and chives. Season to taste with salt and black pepper and cook for 5 minutes, stirring frequently.

3 Pour over 1¼ cups cold water and bring to a boil. Lower the heat, cover the pan and simmer the sauce for 10 minutes.

4 Drain the fish and discard the marinade. Add the fish to the sauce, and cook for 10 minutes, turning the fish from time to time.

5 Pour over the lime juice and wine. Stir in the garlic and bring to a boil. Lower the heat slightly and simmer, uncovered, for 5 minutes. Taste and adjust the seasoning.

6 Remove from the heat and transfer to a warmed serving dish. Sprinkle over the chives and serve the fish immediately.

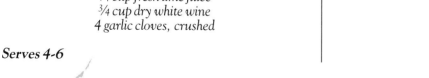

Fish Fillets in a Lime Sauce

A perfect fish for those who are watching their weight, Fish Fillets in a Lime Sauce is both healthy and slimming.

2 lb fish fillets, fluke or sole, skimmed
juice of 1 lime
salt and white pepper
2 tablespoons butter

For the sauce
1 1/4 cups chicken stock
grated rind of 1/2 lime
1 tablespoon cornstarch
juice of 2 limes
2 egg yolks, lightly beaten
1 teaspoon sugar
1 tablespoon minced fresh chives
pinch of ground ginger

For garnish
whole chives
1 lime, halved

Serves 4

1 Wash the fish fillets under cold water. Pat dry with paper towels. Rub the lime juice over the fillets and season with salt and pepper. Roll up the fillets.

2 Grease a large plate with a little of the butter then place the rolled-up fillets on the plate. Dot with the remaining butter. Cover with foil. Place the plate over a saucepan half-filled with boiling water, and steam the fish for 10-15 minutes until cooked.

3 Meanwhile make the sauce: Put the chicken stock and lime rind into a saucepan. Bring to a boil. Lower heat and simmer for 5 minutes. Mix the cornstarch with the lime juice, and add to the stock. Cook over low heat, stirring constantly, for 5 minutes.

4 Put the egg yolks and the sugar in a heatproof bowl and gradually pour over the stock, beating with a wooden spoon as you pour.

5 Place the bowl over a saucepan half-filled with simmering water and cook, stirring, for 5-10 minutes, until sauce thickens. Add ginger and season to taste.

6 Transfer fish to a heated serving platter. Pour over the sauce and garnish with chives and lime halves.

Fish Pie

The sweet potato topping on this Fish Pie provides the perfect contrast to the savory fish filling.

1/2 cup butter
2 tablespoons oil
1 large onion, minced
1 lb white fish fillets, cod or haddock, skinned
1/2 lb salt cod, soaked, skinned and shredded
2 hard-cooked eggs, chopped
1 1/2 lb sweet potatoes
salt and freshly ground black pepper
1/4 cup milk

For the sauce
3 tablespoons butter
2 tablespoons all-purpose flour
1 1/4 cups milk
1 cup shredded Cheddar or Swiss cheese
1 teaspoon curry powder
2 tablespoons minced fresh parsley

Serves 6

1 Melt 2 tablespoons of the butter with the oil in a large skillet over medium heat. Add the onion and sauté for 5 minutes. Add the fish and cook for 8-10 minutes. Remove pan from heat and stir in the eggs. Transfer to an ovenproof dish and set aside.

2 Boil the sweet potatoes in salted water for 15-20 minutes until soft. Drain, then rinse under cold water and peel. Put in a bowl and mash until smooth with 1/4 cup of the butter and the milk. Season to taste.

3 Preheat the oven to 350°F.

4 Make the sauce: Melt the butter in a saucepan, sprinkle in the flour and stir over low heat for 2 minutes. Off heat, gradually stir in the milk. Return pan to heat and bring to a boil. Lower heat and simmer, stirring constantly for 2-3 minutes. Add cheese, curry powder and parsley. Season to taste. Cook for 3-4 minutes more until sauce is thick.

5 Pour the sauce over the fish and mix well. Spoon the puréed sweet potato over the top. Dot with remaining butter; cook in oven for 30 minutes.

Fish fillets in a Lime Sauce and Martinique Poached Fish

Fish Steaks with Orange and Anchovy Butter

The fish called dolphin in the Caribbean bears no resemblance to the friendly dolphin or porpoise!

4 fish steaks, each weighing ½lb, tuna or dolphin

For the marinade
2 garlic cloves, crushed
1 fresh chili, seeded and minced
1 onion, grated
2 tablespoons fresh lime juice
2 tablespoons olive oil
2 teaspoons dried thyme
1 teaspoon salt
freshly ground black pepper

For the butters
⅓ cup soft butter
1 teaspoon grated orange rind
1 teaspoon dried thyme
1 teaspoon minced fresh chives
4 anchovy fillets, rinsed and mashed

For garnish
4 orange slices
4 anchovy fillets, rolled

Serves 4

1 Wash the fish steaks and pat dry on paper towels. Place in a shallow china or glass dish.

2 Make the marinade: Mix the garlic, chili, onion, lime juice, olive oil, thyme, salt and pepper together. Pour over the fish and set aside to marinate for at least 2 hours or overnight, turning from time to time.

3 Make the butters: Mix half the butter with the orange rind, thyme and chives in a small bowl. Shape into a small roll about 1 inch in diameter. Mix the remaining butter with the mashed anchovy and make a roll in the same way. Cover each roll with plastic wrap and freeze for 30 minutes.

4 Remove the butters from the freezer and cut each one in 4 slices. Place on a plate, cover with plastic wrap and chill in the refrigerator until required.

5 Preheat the broiler to high or light the barbecue.

6 Remove the fish steaks from marinade, transfer to the broiler pan or barbecue grill and cook for 8-10 minutes, or until cooked through and golden brown on each side, brushing with the marinade.

7 Put fish on a warmed serving dish, garnished with the orange butter on the orange slices and the rolled anchovies on the anchovy butter. Serve immediately.

Fried Flying Fish

1lb flying fish fillets, skinned
1½ teaspoons salt
juice of 1 lime
1 garlic clove, crushed
1 teaspoon minced fresh chives
1 small onion, minced
½ teaspoon dried marjoram
dash of hot pepper sauce (Tabasco)
⅓ cup all-purpose flour
⅛ teaspoon cayenne
freshly ground black pepper
1 egg, lightly beaten
oil, for panfrying
2 limes, cut in quarters, for garnish

Serves 4

1 Put the fish fillets in a shallow glass or china dish, season with 1 teaspoon salt and the lime juice and set aside for 15 minutes.

2 Drain and pat dry on paper towels. In a small bowl, mix the garlic, chives, onion, marjoram and hot pepper sauce together. Rub mixture into fillets.

3 Mix the flour, cayenne, ½ teaspoon salt and black pepper together in a shallow bowl. Place the beaten egg in another bowl. Dip the fillets first into the egg then into the seasoned flour.

4 Heat the oil in a heavy-bottomed skillet and cook the fillets, a few at a time, for 3 minutes on each side. Keep warm while cooking the remaining fillets.

5 Garnished with lime wedges and serve.

Fish Loaf

An interesting and economical dish, Fish Loaf is ideal for picnics. Serve with crusty French bread, a crisp green salad and lashings of homemade mayonnaise.

1 tablespoon butter, plus 1 teaspoon, for greasing
1 lb white fish fillets, cod, haddock, snapper or lingcod,
skinned
1 tablespoon fresh lime juice
2 onions
1 bay leaf
2 whole cloves
salt and freshly ground black pepper
1 teaspoon whole black peppercorns
1 tablespoon all-purpose flour
1 1/4 cups milk
2 eggs, beaten
2 hard-cooked eggs, chopped
2 tablespoons capers, rinsed
2 tablespoons chopped gherkins
2 tablespoons minced fresh parsley
2 cups soft white bread crumbs
parsley sprigs, for garnish

Serves 4-6

1 Lightly grease a 7×3 inch loaf pan with the 1 teaspoon of butter.

2 Put the fish in a saucepan, add the lime juice and pour over enough cold water to cover. Slice one of the onions and add with the bay leaf, cloves, 1 teaspoon salt and the black peppercorns. Bring to a boil over medium heat. Lower the heat, cover the pan and simmer for 10 minutes or until the fish flakes easily when tested with a fork.

3 Drain the fish and discard the seasonings. Flake the flesh with a fork and set aside.

4 Preheat the oven to 350°F.

5 Heat the 1 tablespoon butter in a saucepan, sprinkle in the flour and cook, stirring constantly, for 2 minutes. Off heat, gradually stir in the milk. Season with salt and pepper to taste.

6 Return the pan to a low heat and cook, stirring constantly with a wooden spoon for 3-5 minutes, until the sauce coats the back of the spoon. Remove pan from heat.

7 Mince the remaining onion and add to the sauce. Stir in the flaked fish, beaten eggs, hard-cooked eggs, capers, gherkins, parsley and bread crumbs. Season to taste with salt and pepper.

8 Spoon the mixture into the prepared pan. Cover with foil and cook in the oven for 45 minutes.

9 Remove from the oven and let cool. Cover with plastic wrap then refrigerate overnight.

10 To serve, unmold the fish loaf by running a knife around the inside of the pan, then invert it on a serving platter. Garnish with parsley sprigs.

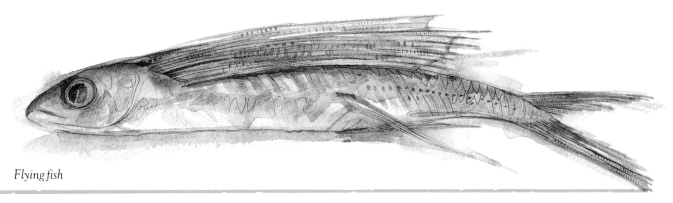

Flying fish

Stuffed and Baked Red Snapper

The red snapper in this recipe is wrapped in bacon before it is cooked to keep the fish succulent.

¼ cup melted butter
2 small red snappers, each weighing 1¼lb, cleaned
8 bacon slices
2 tablespoons olive oil
salt and freshly ground black pepper

For the stuffing
1 small onion, minced
¾ cup minced mushrooms
¾ cup minced ham
1½ cups soft white bread crumbs
1 teaspoon finely grated lemon rind
2 tablespoons minced fresh parsley
1 teaspoon minced fresh thyme
1 egg, lightly beaten

Serves 4

1 Preheat the oven to 350°F.

2 Using 1 tablespoon of the melted butter, lightly grease a large, shallow ovenproof dish.

3 Make the stuffing: Mix the onion, mushrooms, ham, bread crumbs, lemon rind, parsley, thyme and egg together in a large bowl. Season to taste.

4 Enlarge the abdominal cavity of each fish to accommodate the stuffing. Stuff each fish with half the mixture and secure the openings with cocktail picks. Wrap 4 bacon slices around each fish.

5 Place the fish in the prepared ovenproof dish. Pour over the oil and remaining melted butter, and season.

6 Bake in the oven for 40-45 minutes, or until the fish flakes easily when tested with a fork, basting occasionally with the oil and butter.

7 Transfer to a warmed serving dish and serve immediately.

Stewed Shark

Fish in the Caribbean is often rubbed with salt and lime before it is cooked, to "cut the freshness" – a term used to describe the rather strong smell that fish tends to have in hot climates.

2¼lb shark, cut in 1 inch cubes
juice of 1 lime
1 teaspoon salt
1 tablespoon rum
3 tablespoons olive oil
¼lb salt pork, diced
2 large Bermuda onions, finely sliced
3 garlic cloves, crushed
2 sweet red peppers, seeded and finely sliced
1 can (16oz) tomatoes, drained and chopped
1 cup white wine
1 hot seasoning pepper
1 teaspoon dried oregano
1 tablespoon chopped fresh cilantro
salt and freshly ground black pepper

Serves 6

1 Wash the fish cubes under cold water then rub with lime juice and salt. Rinse under cold water.

2 Place the fish in a bowl, pour over the rum and set aside for 10 minutes.

3 Heat the oil in a Dutch oven. Add the diced salt pork and cook for 5 minutes until brown all over. Remove with a slotted spoon. Drain on paper towels.

4 Add the onions to the pot and sauté for 7 minutes until soft. Stir in the garlic and sweet red peppers and cook for 5 minutes.

5 Drain the shark, reserving the liquid, and add the fish to the pot. Cook for 5 minutes, stirring frequently. Pour over the reserved liquid and add the tomatoes, white wine, seasoning pepper, oregano and cilantro. Return the salt pork to the pot and season to taste with salt and pepper. Bring to a boil, then lower the heat, cover the pot and simmer for 30 minutes, stirring frequently.

6 Serve straight from the pot accompanied by Rice 'n' Peas (see page 80).

Stuffed and Baked Red Snapper

Crayfish and Rice Salad

A spectacular dish to serve at a dinner party or as part of a grand buffet, Crayfish and Rice Salad combines the delicate flavor of crayfish with the tropical tastes of pineapple, papaya and rice. Crayfish look very attractive with their scarlet color and long claws but have very little flesh. If they are difficult to obtain or you wish for a more substantial shellfish, use either jumbo shrimp or small lobsters split in half.

1 onion, sliced
1 carrot, sliced
1 bay leaf
3 whole cloves
1 inch piece of fresh gingerroot, pared
1 teaspoon salt
freshly ground black pepper
2¼lb uncooked, freshly-killed crayfish in shells
(12 crayfish)
¼lb fresh young spinach, stems removed
¾ pineapple, pared and sliced
1½ papayas, peeled, seeded and sliced

For the rice
2½ cups long-grain rice, rinsed and drained
4 scallions, trimmed and minced
½ bunch watercress, trimmed and chopped
2 tablespoons minced fresh parsley
2 tablespoons minced fresh cilantro
½ papaya, peeled, seeded and finely chopped
¼ pineapple, pared and chopped
3 tablespoons oil
juice and grated rind of 1 orange
juice of 1 lime
10 whole young spinach leaves

For the mayonnaise
2 egg yolks
1¼ cups olive oil
1 tablespoon ketchup
juice of ½ lime
1 garlic clove, crushed
salt

Serves 6

1 Put the onion, carrot, bay leaf, cloves and ginger into a large saucepan. Pour over 7½ cups of cold water. Add one 1 teaspoon salt and black pepper and bring to a boil over medium heat. Lower the heat, cover the pan and simmer for 10 minutes. Carefully add the crayfish to the pan and bring back to a boil. Lower the heat and simmer for 5 minutes. Off heat, strain the liquor into a liquid measure and reserve. Refresh the crayfish under cold water. Discard the seasonings and let the crayfish cool.

2 Put the rice in a pan, add 2½ cups of the reserved liquor and bring to a boil over medium heat. Lower the heat, cover the pan and simmer for 20 minutes until the rice is tender and the liquid has been absorbed. Remove from the heat, transfer to a mixing bowl and let cool slightly.

3 Add the scallions, watercress, parsley, cilantro, papaya, pineapple, 2 tablespoons oil, orange juice and rind and the lime juice to the rice. Gently toss the ingredients together until they are thoroughly combined.

4 Grease an 8-cup ring mold with the remaining oil. Line the mold with the spinach leaves, overlapping each one slightly. Spoon in the rice, smoothing the top with the back of a spoon. Cover with a plate and chill in the refrigerator for 1 hour.

5 Make the mayonnaise: Beat the egg yolks in a small bowl. Still beating, add the oil, drop by drop, until it starts to thicken, then add the oil in a slow thin stream. When the mixture is thick, stir in the ketchup, lime juice and garlic. Season to taste with salt and black pepper. Pour into a small bowl.

6 Line a large round serving platter with the spinach leaves. Remove the rice from the refrigerator and unmold onto the plate.

7 Put the bowl of mayonnaise in the center of the rice (alternatively, spoon the mayonnaise into the center). Arrange the sliced pineapple and papaya around the rice, then place the whole crayfish in a circle against the rice, with their tails just hanging over the plate. Serve immediately.

Stuffed Crabs
Crab Backs

Stuffed Crabs, or Crab Backs as they are called in Trinidad, make a most delicious dinner party dish. Serve as an appetizer or as a main course accompanied by freshly baked rolls and a crisp green salad.

In the West Indies, Crab Backs are made with the small blue-backed land crabs that live in the mangrove swamps and coconut fields, however the blue crabs from the Atlantic and Gulf coasts are equally suitable.

4 cooked blue crabs, each weighing approximately ¾lb,
split open
2 tablespoons butter
1 onion, minced
3 scallions, trimmed and minced
1 fresh chili, seeded and minced
2 tablespoons minced fresh chives
2 teaspoons Worcestershire sauce
1 tablespoon fresh lime juice
2 tablespoons medium sherry or rum
pinch of grated nutmeg
1 teaspoon salt
freshly ground black pepper
2 cups soft white bread crumbs

Serves 2-4

1 Clean the crabs: Remove and discard the stomach, digestive tract, and the gills (dead man's fingers), and pick out all the crab meat from the shell, discarding any skin or cartilage. Reserve the shells. Crack open the claws and combine all the meat together in a large mixing bowl.

2 Preheat the oven to 350°F.

3 Melt the butter in a skillet, add the onion and scallions and sauté, stirring constantly over medium heat for 5 minutes, until soft and golden.

4 Off heat, stir the onion and scallions into the crab meat. Add the chili, chives, Worcestershire, lime juice, sherry or rum, nutmeg, salt and freshly ground pepper. Stir in 1¾ cups bread crumbs, then mix the ingredients thoroughly together.

5 Spoon the filling into the reserved shells and place on a baking sheet. Cook in the center of the oven for 15 minutes.

6 Remove the crabs from the oven and sprinkle over the remaining bread crumbs. Return to the oven and cook for a further 15-20 minutes, until golden brown. Serve hot.

Pepper Shrimp

A great dish to share with friends – all you need is a dish for the shells and beer to put out the heat!

2 tablespoons olive oil
5 garlic cloves, crushed
2-3 fresh chilies, seeded and minced
2 tablespoons fresh lemon juice
4 tomatoes, peeled and chopped
salt and freshly ground black pepper
1 tablespoon Pepper Wine (see page 95)
36 cooked shrimp, in shells

Serves 6-8

1 Heat the oil in a wok or large heavy-bottomed skillet. Add the garlic and chilies and stir-fry for 1 minute over medium heat.

2 Stir in the lemon juice and tomatoes, and season to taste with salt and pepper. Cook for a further 5 minutes. Add the pepper wine and shrimp and cook for 5 minutes, stirring constantly, to heat through.

3 Transfer contents of pan to a warmed serving dish and serve immediately.

Crab Gumbo

The word "gumbo" is synonymous with okra. This thick soupy stew can be made with crab, meat, fish or poultry, but always has okra as a common ingredient. When buying okra choose the small firm pods and avoid the large dark green pods which tend to be rather tough and stringy.

2 cooked crabs, each weighing 1¼lb, cleaned
2 tablespoons butter
1 tablespoon olive oil
1 Bermuda onion, minced
1 can (16oz) tomatoes, drained and chopped
1 tablespoon minced fresh thyme
2 tablespoons minced fresh parsley
1 tablespoon minced fresh chives
½lb okra, trimmed and sliced
1 hot seasoning pepper
salt and freshly ground black pepper

Serves 4-6

1 Using a cleaver, cut off the legs and claws from the crab and crack with a lobster or nut cracker. Then cut the body into quarters.

2 Heat the butter and the oil together in a large saucepan over medium heat. Add the onion and sauté, stirring constantly for 5 minutes.

3 Add the crab and cook, turning frequently for 5 minutes. Stir in the tomatoes, thyme, parsley and chives and cook, stirring constantly for 5 minutes.

4 Add the okra and hot seasoning pepper and pour over 5 cups boiling water. Season with salt and pepper to taste. Lower the heat and simmer for 45 minutes, stirring occasionally.

5 Remove the hot seasoning pepper, transfer to a warmed soup tureen and serve immediately, ladling the gumbo into soup bowls.

Curried Shrimp and Pineapple

Uncooked (green) shrimp have much better flavor than the pink cooked ones. They are sold fresh at some fish markets and frozen at gourmet stores and oriental supermarkets.

2 small pineapples
1 tablespoon butter
1 tablespoon oil
1 large onion, minced
1½ tablespoons garam masala
¼ teaspoon ground saffron (or turmeric)
pinch of cayenne
16 (green) uncooked jumbo shrimp, shelled,
cut in ½ inch lengths
1 tablespoon fresh lemon juice
1¼ cups heavy cream
1 cup toasted almonds
salt and freshly ground black pepper

Serves 4

1 Cut the pineapples in half lengthwise through the leaves. Using a small sharp knife, cut out the pineapple flesh, and chop in ½ inch cubes. Set aside. Place the hollowed-out pineapple halves on a large serving platter.

2 Melt the butter with the oil in a large skillet over medium heat. Add the onion and sauté for 5 minutes. Stir in the garam masala, saffron and cayenne and cook for a further 2 minutes.

3 Add the shrimp and lemon juice to the skillet and stir-fry for 5 minutes. Pour over the cream, add the pineapple cubes and half the almonds and season to taste with salt and black pepper. Cook for a further 5 minutes, stirring constantly.

4 Remove the skillet from the heat and spoon the mixture into the reserved pineapple shells. Scatter over the remaining almonds and serve immediately.

Pepper Shrimp (front) and Crab Gumbo

Shrimp and Rice
Arroz con Camarones

The combination of shrimp with rice is another inter-island specialty, with each island in the Caribbean having its own version. This particular recipe reflects the Spanish influence in the cooking of the Caribbean.

3 tablespoons olive oil
1 large onion, minced
2 scallions, trimmed and minced
3 garlic cloves, crushed
4 tomatoes, peeled and chopped
1 can (about 14oz) pimientos, drained and sliced
2 tablespoons minced fresh parsley
2 tablespoons minced fresh cilantro
2 cups medium-grain rice, rinsed and drained
salt and freshly ground black pepper
4 cups chicken stock
1 hot seasoning pepper
1 can (16oz) peas, drained
6 cups uncooked (green) shrimp, in shells
2 tablespoons fresh lemon juice
1 avocado, for garnish

Serves 6

1 Heat the oil in a large heavy-bottomed skillet. Add the onion and cook for 5 minutes over medium heat. Stir in the scallions, garlic and tomatoes and cook for 5 minutes, stirring constantly.

2 Add the pimientos, parsley, cilantro and rice. Season to taste with salt and black pepper and cook for 2 minutes, stirring constantly. Pour over the chicken stock, add the seasoning pepper, and bring to a boil. Lower the heat, cover the pan and simmer for 15 minutes.

3 Carefully stir the peas and shrimp into the rice, and cook for a further 10 minutes, turning the shrimp frequently so that they cook evenly.

4 Pour over the lemon juice. Taste and adjust the seasoning. Transfer to a warmed serving dish. Peel and thinly slice the avocado. Garnish with the avocado slices and serve immediately.

Shrimp-filled Edam Cheese
Keshy Yena

One of the most interesting dishes of the Caribbean, Shrimp-filled Edam Cheese or Keshy Yena is a specialty from the Dutch island of Curaçao.

1 whole Edam cheese (about 4lb), wax skin removed
1 tablespoon butter, for greasing

For the filling
1 tablespoon butter
6 scallions, trimmed and minced
1 fresh chili, seeded and minced
1 green pepper, seeded and finely chopped
2 cups shelled cooked shrimp
1/3 cup chopped gherkins
1/3 cup golden raisins
2 tomatoes, peeled and chopped
1 cup soft white bread crumbs
1 teaspoon Worcestershire sauce
1 tablespoon sherry
1 egg, beaten
salt and freshly ground black pepper

Serves 6

1 Slice one inch off the top of the cheese to use for a lid. Carefully scoop out most of the cheese inside the lid and hollow out the whole cheese, leaving a ¾ inch thick shell. Shred the cheese and reserve.

2 Preheat the oven to 350°F. Grease a shallow ovenproof dish with the butter.

3 Make the filling: Melt the butter in a skillet, add the scallions, chili and green pepper and cook for 5 minutes over medium heat, stirring constantly. Off heat, stir in the shrimp, gherkins, golden raisins, tomatoes, bread crumbs, Worcestershire, sherry and egg. Add 1½ cups of the reserved shredded cheese, mix well together and season to taste with salt and black pepper.

4 Pack the cheese with the filling. Cover with the lid, then put in the ovenproof dish and cook in the center of the oven for 30 minutes. (Do not overcook or the cheese will become hard.)

5 Serve immediately from the dish, cutting the cheese in slices.

Seafood Pancakes

A rich and impressive dish for seafood lovers, these delicious pancakes can be made the day before and heated through and filled just before serving.

¼ cup oil, for cooking

For the batter
2 cups all-purpose flour
½ teaspoon salt
¼ teaspoon grated nutmeg
2 eggs, beaten
1 tablespoon oil
2½ cups milk

For the filling
2 tablespoons oil
¼ cup butter
1 onion, minced
2 garlic cloves, crushed
1⅓ cups crab meat
6oz white fish fillets, cod, haddock or pollock, skinned and cut in 1 inch cubes
1½ cups shelled cooked shrimp
⅔ cup white wine
2 tablespoons all-purpose flour
1¼ cups milk
1 ripe avocado
1½ cups shredded Gruyère cheese
⅛ teaspoon grated nutmeg
salt and freshly ground black pepper

For garnish
1 firm ripe avocado
1 lime, thinly sliced

Serves 6 (Makes 12 pancakes)

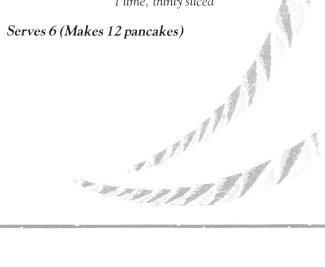

1 First make the batter: Sift the flour, salt and nutmeg into a large mixing bowl. Make a well in the center and add the beaten eggs, oil and 2 tablespoons of the milk. Beat together with a wire whip, gradually drawing in the flour. Slowly pour in the remaining milk and ½ cup water, and beat the mixture into a smooth batter. Let stand for 30 minutes.

2 Meanwhile make the filling: Heat the oil with 2 tablespoons butter in a large skillet over medium heat. Add the onion and sauté, stirring constantly for 5 minutes. Stir in the garlic and cook for 3 minutes.

3 Add the crab meat to the pan and stir-fry for 6 minutes. Add the fish, shrimp and the white wine and cook for 10 minutes, stirring constantly, until the fish is cooked and most of the liquid has been absorbed. Remove from the heat and set aside.

4 Melt the remaining butter in a saucepan over medium heat. Sprinkle over the flour and cook, stirring constantly, for 2 minutes.

5 Off heat, gradually add the milk, stirring constantly. Peel the avocado and mash to a purée, then stir into the sauce with the cheese and nutmeg. Season to taste.

6 Return to low heat and cook for 5 minutes, stirring constantly, until the mixture is thick enough to coat the back of the spoon. Stir in the seafood mixture and keep warm while you make the pancakes.

7 Heat an 8 inch skillet over moderately high heat. Pour in 1 teaspoon of the oil and wipe over the skillet with paper towels. Pour in three-fourths of a ladle of the batter, tipping the pan as you pour, so the batter evenly coats the base.

8 Cook for approximately 30 seconds, until the surface sets and the bottom of the pancake is golden brown. Using a spatula, turn the pancake over and cook for 30 seconds. Keep warm in a low oven while you cook the remaining batter. Adjust the heat under the skillet for each pancake.

9 Divide the filling equally among the pancakes and roll them up. Arrange on a warmed serving dish. Peel and thinly slice the avocado, then garnish with the avocado and lime slices and serve immediately.

MEAT DISHES

Since chicken, pigs and goats are easy to rear in the Caribbean climate, they provide the most popular form of meat on most of the islands. However, for those with a taste for wild game, there is plenty of local game still hunted; agouti, armadillo and even parrot are said to be eaten on some islands. All meat is either marinated and seasoned before it is cooked or highly seasoned during cooking, making it very tasty.

Chicken in Coconuts

A novel way to serve Chicken in Coconuts is to place the coconut halves on a bed of rice to prevent them from toppling over. The rice can be decorated with mango and sprigs of cilantro.

3 coconuts, drained and liquid reserved
1 tablespoon butter
1 tablespoon olive oil
2 garlic cloves, crushed
2¼lb skinned chicken cut in 1 inch cubes (about 6 cups)
1 onion, minced
1 teaspoon minced fresh gingerroot
1 tablespoon minced fresh cilantro
1 teaspoon salt
pinch of white pepper
1 tablespoon cornstarch
⅔ cup light cream
1 large firm ripe mango, peeled and diced
finely chopped fresh cilantro, for garnish

Serves 6

1 Split the coconuts in half, scoop out the flesh and cut away the brown skin from half a coconut. Cut into thin slivers with a vegetable parer and reserve. Make thick rich coconut milk using all the remaining coconut flesh (see page 16). Reserve 2½ cups for this recipe (freeze the rest). Put the 6 coconut halves into a serving dish.

2 Preheat the broiler to medium and sprinkle the slivered coconut into the broiler pan. Toast under the broiler for 5-10 minutes, shaking the pan frequently, until the coconut is golden brown. Transfer to a bowl and set aside.

3 Heat the butter and oil together in a saucepan. Add the garlic and cook for 1 minute. Stir in the chicken cubes and cook for 5 minutes, stirring frequently. Using a slotted spoon, transfer the chicken to a plate.

4 Add the onion and gingerroot to the pan and cook for 5 minutes. Pour in the coconut milk and cilantro. Return the chicken to the pan, season with the salt and white pepper and bring to a boil. Lower the heat, cover the pan and simmer for 15 minutes.

5 Mix the cornstarch with 3 tablespoons of the cream. Add the cornstarch mixture, remaining cream and mango to the pan and cook for 2 minutes, or until the sauce is smooth and fairly thick. Stir in the toasted coconut and spoon the chicken mixture into the 6 coconut shells. Finish with a sprinkling of minced cilantro.

Chicken in Coconuts

Chicken and Hearts of Palm Pie

This recipe came originally from South America, and through the years has been changed and adapted to the Caribbean islands. The pastry is very crumbly and has to be pieced together like a patchwork. It is a good dish to eat cold at picnics.

5 cups all-purpose flour
pinch of salt
¼ teaspoon grated nutmeg
3 eggs, beaten
1 tablespoon melted butter
1-1¼ cups oil, plus 1 teaspoon, for greasing
1 egg yolk, lightly beaten, for glazing

For the filling
2 tablespoons butter
2 tablespoons all-purpose flour
1¼ cups milk
salt and freshly ground black pepper
1 bay leaf
1 tablespoon oil
1 large onion, minced
2 garlic cloves, crushed
2 tomatoes, peeled and chopped
1 can (16oz) hearts of palm, drained and cut in ½ inch lengths
1 can (16oz) peas, drained
3 cups skinned cooked chicken in ½ inch cubes
2 tablespoons minced fresh parsley

Serves 6

1 First make the filling: Melt the butter in a saucepan over medium heat. Sprinkle over the flour and cook, stirring constantly for 2 minutes.

2 Off heat, gradually add the milk, stirring constantly. Season to taste with the salt and pepper and add the bay leaf. Return to low heat and cook for 5 minutes, stirring constantly, until the sauce is thick enough to coat the back of the spoon. Remove the bay leaf and set aside.

3 Heat the oil in another saucepan, add the onion and sauté over medium heat for 5 minutes, until soft and golden. Stir in the garlic and tomatoes and cook for 3 minutes. Add the hearts of palm, peas, chicken and parsley. Season to taste with salt and black pepper.

4 Stir the mixture into the sauce and let cool completely.

5 Meanwhile make the pastry: Put the flour, salt and nutmeg into a large mixing bowl. Make a well in the center and add the eggs, butter and 1 cup oil, adding more oil if the mixture seems dry. Form the mixture into a dough with your hands.

6 Preheat the oven to 350°F. Lightly grease an 8 × 10 inch rectangular pie dish with the teaspoon of oil.

7 Roll out half the pastry on a floured surface until it is ¼ inch thick. Lift pieces of the crumbly pastry with a spatula and piece them together in the pie dish, pressing the edges together. Completely line the pie dish then spoon in the chicken filling.

8 Roll out the remaining pastry in the same way and cover the filling, sealing the edges with your fingers. Roll out the pastry trimmings and decorate the top of the pie. Brush the top with the beaten egg yolk and place the pie in the center of the oven for 45-60 minutes, until the crust is golden brown.

9 Remove from the oven and serve immediately.

Chicken Fricassée

This French Creole chicken stew is one of the characteristic dishes of the Caribbean. Take care when caramelizing the sugar not to let it burn.

3½lb broiler-fryer, cut in 12 pieces
1 tablespoon oil
1 tablespoon dark brown sugar
2 onions, minced
4 scallions, trimmed and minced
3 tomatoes, peeled and chopped
2 cups chicken stock
1 hot seasoning pepper
1 bay leaf
2 tablespoons minced fresh parsley, for garnish

For the marinade
juice of 1 lime
2 garlic cloves
1 teaspoon dried thyme
1 fresh chili, seeded and minced
1 tablespoon Worcestershire sauce
salt and freshly ground black pepper

Serves 6

1 Make the marinade: Mix all the marinade ingredients together in a small bowl.

2 Put the chicken pieces in a large mixing bowl and pour over the marinade. Marinate for 2 hours, turning occasionally. Drain, reserving marinade.

3 In a large saucepan or Dutch oven carefully heat the oil and sugar over medium heat until the sugar begins to caramelize. Add half the chicken at a time and brown for 15 minutes, turning frequently. Remove with a slotted spoon.

4 Sauté the onions and scallions for 5 minutes in the oil remaining in the pan, stirring frequently.

5 Stir in the tomatoes and cook for 5 minutes. Pour over the stock and the reserved marinade, then add the seasoning pepper and bay leaf and bring to a boil. Return chicken to pan and lower heat. Simmer for 20-30 minutes, or until the chicken is tender. Taste and adjust seasoning.

6 To serve, transfer the chicken and sauce to a warmed serving dish, remove the seasoning pepper and bay leaf and garnish with parsley.

Banana and Rice Stuffed Chicken

The sweet stuffing of bananas and rice goes perfectly with the succulent flesh of the roast chicken. This recipe is an adaptation of a famous Haitian recipe where the chicken is flambéed in rum as it is served.

4lb roasting chicken
1 teaspoon salt
¼ teaspoon white pepper
1 tablespoon honey
¼ cup fresh orange juice
watercress sprigs, for garnish

For the stuffing
1½ cups cooked rice
3 ripe bananas, mashed
juice and grated rind of 1 large orange
1 tablespoon rum
2 tablespoons golden raisins
pinch of ground ginger
pinch of grated nutmeg
salt and freshly ground black pepper

Serves 6

1 Preheat the oven to 350°F.

2 Make the stuffing: Mix the rice, bananas, orange juice and rind, rum, golden raisins, ginger and nutmeg together. Season to taste with salt and black pepper.

3 Wash the chicken and dry with paper towels. Fill the cavity of the chicken with the stuffing. Season the outside with the salt and white pepper and place in a roasting pan.

4 Mix the honey with the orange juice and pour over the chicken.

5 Roast in the oven for 1½ hours, basting occasionally, until the chicken is tender and cooked through when tested with a skewer.

6 Transfer to a warmed serving dish, garnish with watercress sprigs and serve immediately.

Chicken with Rice and Pigeon Peas
Chicken Pelau

Each island in the Caribbean has its own way of seasoning, depending upon which herbs grow locally. The seasoning herbs are generally combined with onion, garlic, sive or chives and sometimes a little hot pepper, then blended to a purée with a little water. The mixture is then kept in a screw-top jar in the refrigerator and used each day.

Chicken Pelau is a national favorite in Trinidad and Tobago. Most people will eat a pelau on a Sunday after coming back from the beach.

A good pelau must be brown – the secret lies in "browning down" or caramelizing the chicken in a little oil and sugar to give it that rich brown color.

½ coconut, chopped
liquid from the coconut
1 can (16oz) pigeon peas, drained
1 hot seasoning pepper
1 teaspoon salt
freshly ground black pepper
2 tablespoons oil
2 tablespoons sugar
3½lb broiler-fryer, cut in 2 inch pieces
1¼ cups rice, rinsed and drained

For the seasoning
1 onion, chopped
2 garlic cloves
1 tablespoon chopped fresh chives
1 tablespoon chopped fresh thyme
2 celery stalks with leaves, chopped

Serves 6

1 Make the seasoning: Put the onion, garlic, chives, thyme and celery into a blender or food processor with ¼ cup water and process for 30 seconds until the mixture is puréed. Pour the seasoning into a pan and set aside while you make the coconut milk.

2 Rinse out the blender or food processor then add the chopped coconut with the coconut liquid and work to a thick milk, adding more water if necessary. Pour into the saucepan, adding the pigeon peas and the seasoning pepper, and place over low heat for 15 minutes. Season with salt and pepper.

3 In a heavy-bottomed saucepan or Dutch oven heat the oil and sugar together over medium heat until the sugar begins to caramelize, taking care not to burn it. Add the chicken pieces and cook for 15-20 minutes, turning frequently, until they are browned all over.

4 Stir in the pigeon pea mixture and the rice, adding 1¼ cups of water. Bring to a boil, then reduce the heat to low, cover the pan and simmer for 20 minutes, until the chicken and rice are cooked.

5 Taste and adjust the seasoning. Discard the hot seasoning pepper before serving.

Chicken with Rice and Pigeon Peas (front) and Banana and Rice Stuffed Chicken

Four-Stuffing Christmas Turkey

In the Caribbean the stuffing is as important as the turkey itself. Impress your family and friends at Christmas time or Thanksgiving with this four-stuffing turkey. Two of the stuffings are hot and two are served together cold like a layered pâté.

15lb turkey, cleaned, washed and dried
1 teaspoon salt
freshly ground black pepper
1 cup melted butter
reserved pineapple juice (see below)

For the Prune and Sausage meat Stuffing
2 tablespoons minced onion
2 tablespoons minced fresh chives
2 tablespoons minced fresh parsley
1½ cups pre-soaked pitted prunes, chopped
1½lb sausage meat
grated rind of 1 orange
1 tablespoon brandy
¼ teaspoon ground cloves
1 teaspoon salt

For the Pineapple and Herb Stuffing
1 large Bermuda onion, minced
6 scallions, minced
3 garlic cloves, crushed
6 cups soft white bread crumbs
2 tablespoons chopped fresh thyme
2 tablespoons minced celery
grated rind and juice of 1 lime
1 can (16oz) pineapple cubes, drained and chopped,
juice reserved (see above)
1 egg, lightly beaten
1 teaspoon salt

For the Chicken Liver Stuffing
1 tablespoon butter
1 tablespoon olive oil
1 onion, minced
3 garlic cloves, crushed
1lb chicken livers, trimmed
½ package (8oz size) cream cheese
½ teaspoon minced fresh basil
1 tablespoon sherry
1 teaspoon salt
2 cups soft white bread crumbs

For the Olive Stuffing
2½ cups ripe pitted olives, minced
3 garlic cloves, crushed
¼ cup butter
1 cup finely ground almonds

For garnish
1½ cups pre-soaked pitted prunes
1 can (16oz) can pineapple rings, drained
watercress sprigs

Serves 12-14

1 Make the Prune and Sausage meat Stuffing: Mix the minced onion, chives, parsley, prunes, sausage meat, orange rind, brandy, cloves, salt and some black pepper together in a large mixing bowl, until thoroughly combined. Set aside.

2 Make the Pineapple and Herb Stuffing: Mix the onion, scallions, garlic, bread crumbs, thyme, celery, grated lime rind and juice, chopped pineapple, egg, salt and some black pepper together in a mixing bowl until they are thoroughly combined. Set aside.

3 Make the Chicken Liver Stuffing: Heat the butter and the oil together in a small skillet. Add the onion and cook over medium heat for 5 minutes, stirring frequently. Stir in the garlic and livers and cook for 8 minutes until the livers are browned on the outside and pink on the inside.

4 Remove from the heat and transfer to a blender or food processor. Add the cream cheese, basil, sherry, salt, some black pepper and the bread crumbs and work until the mixture forms a smooth purée. Set aside.

5 Make the Olive Stuffing: Put the olives, garlic and butter into a blender or food processor and work to a smooth purée. Stir in the finely ground almonds and spoon the mixture into the bottom of a terrine, smoothing down with the back of the spoon.

6 Spoon the chicken liver stuffing into the terrine on top of the olive stuffing and smooth the top with the back of a spoon. Cover and place in the refrigerator.

7 Preheat the oven to 475°F.

8 Stuff the turkey with the Prune and Sausage meat and the Pineapple and Herb Stuffings. Sew up the neck opening with a needle and thread.

9 Line a large roasting pan with two large sheets of foil, with enough overlapping to completely cover the turkey. Place the turkey in the pan and season with salt and pepper. Pour over half of the melted butter, pull up the foil to cover the turkey and fold over the edges to make a package.

10 Place in the oven and cook for 30 minutes.

11 Soak a thin piece of unbleached muslin in the remaining butter. Open the foil and cover the breast, legs and wings of the turkey with the muslin. Reseal the foil, lower the heat to 350°F and cook for a further 3½ hours, basting frequently.

12 Fold back the foil, remove the muslin and pour over the reserved pineapple juice. Cook for 30-45 minutes, basting frequently, or until the bird is golden brown and the juices run clear when a thigh is pierced with the point of a knife.

13 Remove the bird from the oven and transfer to a warmed platter. Garnish with the prunes and pineapple rings and let stand for 15 minutes before carving.

14 Meanwhile, remove the terrine from the refrigerator. Unmold the stuffings on to a large plate. Cut into 12-14 slices, garnish with the watercress and serve with the hot turkey.

Barbecued Chicken Wings

I first ate this dish at a midnight barbecue on a beach in Barbados. It tastes just as good at midday on a hibachi at home and is a favorite with children!

12 chicken wings

For the marinade
½ cup soy sauce
¼ cup ketchup
¼ cup vinegar
¼ cup honey
1 teaspoon ground ginger
freshly ground black pepper

Serves 4-6

1 Make the marinade: Put the soy sauce, ketchup, vinegar, honey, ginger and black pepper into a bowl and mix well.

2 Wash the chicken wings and remove any feathers. Place in a glass or china dish. Pour over the marinade, ensuring that all the wings are coated with the mixture. Cover with plastic wrap and refrigerate for at least 2 hours or overnight.

3 Preheat the oven to 350°F. Transfer the wings to an ovenproof dish, pour over the marinade and cook in the oven for 30 minutes, turning the wings after 15 minutes.

4 Preheat the broiler to medium or light the barbecue.

5 Remove the wings from the oven, drain the marinade and reserve. Place the wings on the broiler pan or barbecue grill and cook for 5-10 minutes, brushing with the reserved marinade, until brown and crispy.

6 Transfer to a warmed serving platter and serve the chicken immediately.

Caribbean Kabobs

A tasty sweet and savory combination, Caribbean Kabobs should be served with Rice 'n' Peas (see page 80) and Okra in Spicy Tomato and Garlic Sauce (see page 82). Mangoes and papayas can be used instead of the bananas.

1 lb pork chops, trimmed and cut in 1½ inch cubes
3 large bananas
12 bacon slices
1 can (16 oz) can pineapple cubes, drained and juice reserved (see below)
1 green pepper, seeded and cut in 1½ inch cubes
1 sweet red pepper, seeded and cut in 1½ inch cubes

For the marinade
1 tablespoon honey
1 tablespoon soy sauce
2 garlic cloves, crushed
reserved pineapple juice (see above)
dash of Angostura bitters

Serves 6

1 First make the marinade: Mix the honey, soy sauce, garlic, reserved pineapple juice and Angostura bitters together in a small bowl.

2 Place the pork cubes in a glass or china dish and pour over the marinade. Set aside to marinate for at least 2 hours or overnight, turning occasionally.

3 Drain the pork cubes and reserve the marinade.

4 Cut each banana in 4 equal lengths. Then roll each piece in a slice of bacon.

5 Preheat the broiler to high.

6 Thread 6 long kabob skewers with alternate pieces of sweet red pepper, pork, green pepper, pork, pineapple, banana and so on, putting 2 pieces of banana on each skewer.

7 Line a broiler pan with foil and place the skewers in the pan. Brush the skewers with the reserved marinade and cook under the broiler for 10 minutes, turning from time to time, and brushing frequently with the marinade, until the meat is cooked.

8 Transfer to a warmed serving platter and serve the kabobs immediately.

Pork with Eggplant

Pork with Eggplant is characteristic of the East Indian influence in West Indian cooking. Local names for eggplant may include melongene and garden egg.

3 tablespoons oil
2 tablespoons sugar
1 lb stew pork, cut in 1 inch cubes
1 onion, minced
2 garlic cloves, crushed
2 teaspoons ground cumin
1 lb eggplant, cut in 1 inch cubes
1 lb potatoes, peeled and cut into 1 inch cubes
1 teaspoon salt
freshly ground black pepper
2½ cups chicken stock

Serves 6

1 Heat 2 tablespoons of the oil with the sugar in a Dutch oven over medium heat until the sugar begins to caramelize. Be careful not to let the sugar burn.

2 Add the pork cubes and cook for 6-8 minutes, stirring constantly, until they are golden brown. Remove with a slotted spoon and set aside.

3 Pour the remaining oil into the pot, add the onion and cook, stirring constantly, over medium heat for 3-5 minutes.

4 Add the garlic, cumin, eggplant and potatoes. Season with salt and pepper and cook for 5 minutes. Return the pork to the pot, pour over the stock and bring to a boil. Lower the heat, cover the pot and simmer, stirring occasionally, for 1 hour until tender.

5 Taste and adjust seasoning. Serve at once, straight from the pot.

Caribbean Kabobs (front) and Pineapple Spare Ribs

Guava Pork Chops

Guavas are one of the most common fruit of the West Indies. When ripe they have a distinctive smell and exotic flavor. They may be eaten raw but are best stewed or made into jelly or guava cheese (a compressed pulp).

4 large pork chops
1 teaspoon dried rosemary
2 garlic cloves
salt and freshly ground black pepper
juice of 1 lemon
2 tablespoons guava jelly
1 can (16oz) guavas, drained and juice reserved
1 tablespoon cornstarch
parsley sprigs, for garnish

For the stuffing
1 small onion, minced
1 cup soft white bread crumbs
1 teaspoon dried rosemary
1 tablespoon minced fresh parsley
1 tablespoon rum
1 tablespoon butter

Serves 4

1 Season the chops with the rosemary, garlic, salt and pepper and set aside.

2 Put the lemon juice, guava jelly and the reserved guava juice in a small saucepan. Place the pan over low heat and cook, stirring constantly for 2 minutes, until the jelly as melted. Remove from the heat.

3 Preheat the broiler to medium.

4 Make the stuffing: Mix the onion, bread crumbs, rosemary, parsley and rum together. Season to taste with salt and pepper.

5 Using a teaspoon, scoop out and discard the seeds from the center of 4 guava halves. Fill the cavities with the stuffing and dot each one with a little of the butter.

6 Line a broiler pan with foil and place the chops and the guavas in the pan. Brush a little of the guava juice over the chops and cook for 10 minutes on each side, brushing frequently with the juice.

7 Remove the guavas after the first 10 minutes, transfer to a serving dish and keep warm in a preheated oven.

8 Switch the broiler to high and cook the chops for about 5 more minutes on each side, until they are golden brown.

9 Transfer the chops to the serving dish and keep warm in the oven while you make the sauce.

10 Pour the cooking juices from the broiler pan into the melted jelly mixture. Blend the cornstarch with 3 tablespoons of the mixture in a small bowl. Add to the pan and bring to a boil over medium heat, stirring constantly. Lower the heat and cook for 1 minute, until the sauce has thickened. Remove from the heat and pour over the chops. Garnish with parsley and serve immediately.

Jerked Pork Chops

Jerked Pork is one of the most famous of the traditional Jamaican dishes. It is thought to have originated from the Caribs and Arawaks and the tradition was carried on by the Maroons (the runaway slaves) who would season and spice a whole pig then roast it over freshly cut twigs.

4 pork chops
parsley sprigs or fresh cilantro, for garnish

For the paste
6 scallions, trimmed and chopped
1 teaspoon minced, seeded hot seasoning pepper
1 teaspoon ground cinnamon
½ teaspoon grated nutmeg
½ teaspoon ground allspice
½ teaspoon ground cloves
1 bay leaf, crumbled
1 tablespoon olive oil
1 teaspoon salt
freshly ground black pepper

Serves 4

1 Make the paste: Put the scallions, seasoning pepper, cinnamon, nutmeg, allspice, cloves, bay leaf, olive oil, salt and pepper into a blender or food processor and work for 30 seconds to a smooth purée. Alternatively, pound the paste ingredients together with a pestle and mortar.

2 Put the pork chops in a large shallow china or glass dish and rub them all over with the paste. Cover with plastic wrap and refrigerate for at least 2 hours or overnight.

3 Preheat the broiler to high.

4 Place the chops on a broiler pan and cook under the broiler for 7-10 minutes on each side.

5 Transfer to a warmed serving platter, garnish with the parsley sprigs or cilantro leaves and serve the chops immediately.

Pineapple Spare Ribs

Molasses, a by-product of sugar cane, is used a great deal in the Caribbean. The molasses in this recipe gives the ribs a distinctive flavor and rich brown color.

2¼lb country-style pork spare ribs, trimmed
½ cup malt vinegar
4 tablespoons cornstarch
2 tablespoons molasses
½ cup oil

For the sauce
1 can (16oz) pineapple cubes
2 tablespoons honey
2 tablespoons dark brown sugar
1 cup malt vinegar
1 sweet red pepper, seeded and cut in 1 inch diamonds

Serves 4-6

1 Cut the spare ribs into individual ribs, then using a cleaver cut each rib in half.

2 Put the ribs in a saucepan, pour over the vinegar and 5 cups water. Bring to a boil over medium heat, then lower the heat and simmer for 15 minutes. Drain and cool slightly.

3 Mix the cornstarch and molasses together in a large mixing bowl, add the ribs and coat them with the mixture, using your fingers.

4 Heat the oil in a deep-sided skillet or wok. When the oil is hot, add the ribs a few at a time and cook for 5 minutes, until golden brown. Remove with a slotted spoon and transfer to a plate while cooking the remaining ribs.

5 Make the sauce: Drain the pineapple cubes and pour the juice into a large saucepan. Add the honey, sugar, vinegar and 1 cup water and heat slowly until the honey and sugar have dissolved.

6 Add the spare ribs and bring to a boil. Lower the heat, cover the pan and simmer gently for 30 minutes, turning the ribs frequently. Add the pineapple cubes and sweet red pepper and cook for 5 minutes to heat through.

7 Transfer the contents of the pan to a warmed serving dish and serve immediately.

Beef and Okra Stew
Beef Gumbo

Okra combined with coconut gives this stew a rich and tasty sauce. Serve Beef Gumbo with plain cooked rice and an orange and cucumber salad.

Okra is a popular vegetable in both Creole and Caribbean cooking. When cooked, the pods become sticky and syrupy and are used to thicken soups and stews.

1lb stew beef, cut in 1 inch cubes
salt and freshly ground black pepper
½ teaspoon ground mace
⅓ cup oil
½lb okra, trimmed
1 onion, minced
2 garlic cloves, crushed
4 tomatoes, peeled and chopped
1 cup coconut milk (see page 16)

For garnish
cherry tomatoes (optional)
cilantro sprigs

Serves 4

1 Wipe the meat, and dry on paper towels. Season with ½ teaspoon salt, pepper and the mace.

2 Heat 2 tablespoons oil in a Dutch oven. Add meat and cook for 6 minutes, stirring frequently, until cubes are lightly browned. Remove with a slotted spoon.

3 Wipe out the pot and add 2 tablespoons oil. Add the okra and cook for 5 minutes until brown, stirring frequently. Remove with a slotted spoon.

4 Heat the remaining oil in the pot and gently cook the onion and garlic over low heat for 5 minutes until soft and golden. Add the tomatoes and cook for 3 minutes, stirring constantly.

5 Return the meat and okra to the pot, pour in the coconut milk and 1 cup water. Season with salt and pepper to taste and bring to a boil. Lower the heat, cover the pot and simmer for 2 hours or until the meat is tender.

6 Transfer to a warmed serving dish, garnish with cherry tomatoes, if wished, and cilantro.

Ground Beef Hash
Picadillo

Ground Beef Hash or Picadillo as it is known in Cuba is traditionally served with a fried egg on top. Serve with Black Beans and Rice (see page 78) and a green salad.

2 tablespoons oil
2 onions, minced
1½lb ground beef
1 fresh chili, seeded and minced
2 garlic cloves, crushed
1 green pepper, seeded and chopped
1 sweet red pepper, seeded and chopped
4 tomatoes, peeled and chopped
2 tablespoons minced fresh parsley
½ teaspoon cumin seeds
2 teaspoons dried oregano
¼ teaspoon ground cloves
2 tablespoons golden raisins
1 teaspoon salt
freshly ground black pepper
3 tablespoons chopped stuffed green olives
2 tablespoons capers, rinsed

For garnish
12 whole stuffed green olives, halved
parsley sprigs

Serves 6

1 Heat the oil in a large heavy-bottomed skillet. Add the onions and cook over medium heat for 6 minutes until golden brown.

2 Add the meat and cook, stirring constantly, for 10 minutes until lightly colored.

3 Add the chili, garlic, green and sweet red peppers, tomatoes, parsley, cumin, oregano, cloves, golden raisins, salt and black pepper, and cook for 15 minutes, stirring frequently.

4 Stir in the chopped olives and capers and cook for a further 5 minutes. Taste and adjust the seasoning. Transfer to a warmed serving dish, garnish with the olives and serve immediately.

Ground Beef Hash (front) and Beef and Okra Stew

Stuffed Baked Papaya

This recipe would traditionally be made with green papayas which are used as a vegetable in the Caribbean. The papayas in this version are ripe, providing a sweet contrast to the savory stuffing. Unripe papayas contain an enzyme in the skin which may cause allergic reaction, so it is advisable to wear rubber gloves when handling them.

2 small papayas, total weight about 1½lb, cut in half
lengthwise and seeded
1 lime, quartered, for garnish

For the filling
2 tablespoons oil
6 scallions, trimmed and minced
1 garlic clove, crushed
10oz ground beef (about 1¼ cups)
1 fresh chili, seeded and minced
2 tomatoes, peeled and chopped
2 tablespoons golden raisins
½ cup cashews, toasted and chopped
2 tablespoons grated Parmesan cheese
1 teaspoon salt
freshly ground black pepper

Serves 4

1 Preheat the oven to 350°F.

2 Make the filling: Heat the oil in a skillet, add the scallions and sauté over medium heat for 5 minutes, until soft and golden.

3 Add the garlic and cook for 2 minutes. Stir in the beef and cook for 6-8 minutes until brown.

4 Add the chili, tomatoes, golden raisins and cashews and stir-fry for 5 minutes, or until most of the liquid in the pan has evaporated.

5 Off heat, stir 1 tablespoon of the cheese into the mixture.

6 Spoon the mixture into the papaya shells and place in a shallow roasting pan. Pour enough boiling water into the pan to come one-fourth of the way up the papayas. Sprinkle over the remaining cheese and bake in the oven for 30 minutes.

7 Transfer to individual plates, and serve garnished with lime quarters.

Sweet and Sour Meat Balls

Pounding the meat makes these Sweet and Sour Meat Balls exceptionally light and a great family favorite.

1½lb ground beef
2 cups soft white bread crumbs
2 eggs, lightly beaten
1 onion, minced
1 teaspoon salt
freshly ground black pepper
¼ cup oil

For the sauce
3 celery stalks, thinly sliced
1 green pepper, seeded and thinly sliced
1 sweet red pepper, seeded and thinly sliced
1¾ cups malt vinegar
½ cup packed dark brown sugar
1 tablespoon soy sauce
½ teaspoon salt
1½ tablespoons cornstarch mixed with 2 tablespoons
water
1 can (16oz) pineapple cubes, drained

Serves 6

1 Mix the ground beef, bread crumbs, eggs, onion, salt and black pepper together in a large mixing bowl. Pound the mixture with the palm of your hand for 5 minutes. Shape into golf-ball size meat balls and set aside on a large plate.

2 Heat the oil in a large skillet over medium heat. Add the meat balls, a few at a time, and cook for 6-8 minutes until they are golden brown, turning them frequently. Remove with a slotted spoon and set aside while cooking the remaining meat balls.

3 Make the sauce: Add the celery and peppers to the juices in the skillet and cook for 5 minutes.

4 Mix the vinegar, sugar, soy sauce, salt, cornstarch mix and 1½ cups water together in a bowl. Pour the mixture into the skillet and bring to a boil, stirring constantly. Lower the heat and simmer for 3 minutes.

5 Return the meat balls to the skillet together with the pineapple and cook for a further 20 minutes.

6 Transfer meat balls and sauce to a warmed serving dish and serve immediately.

Gingered Barbecued Lamb

Outdoor eating is a way of life in the Caribbean, and barbecues are a popular way of entertaining. This dish can be cooked to perfection on a barbecue as well as in the oven.

If using an uncovered barbecue, precook the meat in the oven following steps 1-5 for just 45 minutes, then transfer to the barbecue for the remaining cooking time, brushing frequently with the marinade.

Leg of pork can also be cooked in this way.

3½lb leg of lamb
4 garlic cloves, thinly sliced
2 inch piece of fresh gingerroot, pared and thinly sliced
watercress sprigs, for garnish

For the marinade
1¼ cups ketchup
2 tablespoons honey
3 tablespoons Worcestershire sauce
1 teaspoon hot mustard
juice of ½ lemon or lime
⅛ teaspoon cayenne
1 teaspoon salt
freshly ground black pepper

Serves 6-8

1 Make the marinade: Put the ketchup, honey, Worcestershire, mustard, lemon or lime juice, cayenne, salt, freshly ground black pepper and ¾ cup water into a small saucepan and bring to a boil, stirring constantly. Remove from the heat and let to cool.

2 Using a small sharp knife make small incisions all over the leg of lamb and push slivers of the garlic and ginger into the incisions.

3 Place the lamb in a large glass or china ovenproof dish, pour over the marinade and place in the refrigerator for at least 2 hours, turning the lamb once during this time.

4 Preheat the oven to 375°F.

5 Roast the lamb in the dish with the marinade in the center of the oven for 1½ hours, basting from time to time. If the sauce looks too thick add a little more water midway through the cooking time.

6 Remove the lamb from the oven and transfer to a warmed serving dish. Garnish with watercress. Pour off excess oil from the remaining sauce in the pan, then pour into a serving bowl and pass separately.

Plantation Stew
Sancoche

This dish, sometimes served as a soup, was most probably created by slaves who, with their meager ration, used their imaginations to create a tasty meal.

½lb salt beef, cut in 1 inch cubes
½lb salt pork, cut in 1 inch cubes
1 salted pig's tail, cubed or sliced
¼-⅓ cup oil
9oz stew beef, cut in 1 inch cubes
2 onions, chopped
1 cup lentils or split peas, rinsed and drained
½lb green bananas, peeled and cut in 1 inch slices
½lb yam, peeled and cut in 1 inch slices
½lb sweet potatoes, peeled and cut in 1 inch slices
¼lb okra, trimmed
1 hot seasoning pepper
1 teaspoon salt
freshly ground black pepper

Serves 6

1 Put the salt beef, salt pork and salted pig's tail in a large bowl. Pour over enough cold water to cover and let soak for 1 hour. Drain and pat the meat dry with paper towels.

2 Heat 2 tablespoons of the oil in a large saucepan or casserole and cook the salt beef for 6-8 minutes, stirring frequently, until it is lightly colored on all sides. Remove with a slotted spoon and transfer to a plate while browning the rest of the meat, adding more oil if necessary. Set aside.

3 Add 2 tablespoons of oil to the fat in the pan and sauté the onions over medium heat for 5 minutes.

4 Return the meat to the pan, add the lentils or split peas and pour over 2½ cups water. Bring to a boil over medium heat, lower the heat, cover the pan and simmer for 1½ hours.

5 Add the green bananas, yam, sweet potatoes, okra, seasoning pepper, salt and black pepper and cook for a further 20-30 minutes until all is tender.

6 Remove the seasoning pepper and transfer to a warmed serving dish.

Curried Lamb with Lentils

This fairly dry lamb curry is often made with goat and is popular in Trinidad as a spicy filling for roti (Indian bread).

2 tablespoons oil
1½ tablespoons cumin seeds
1 teaspoon turmeric
1 large onion, minced
2 garlic cloves, crushed
1 fresh chili, seeded and chopped
2 inch piece of fresh gingerroot, pared and minced
2¼lb boneless lamb neck slices, cut in 1 inch cubes
1 cup lentils, rinsed and drained
1 can (16oz) tomatoes, drained and chopped
1 teaspoon salt
freshly ground black pepper

Serves 4-6

1 Heat the oil in a Dutch oven, add the cumin and turmeric and cook over medium heat for 1 minute, stirring constantly.

2 Add the onion and cook for 5 minutes. Stir in the garlic, chili and fresh gingerroot and cook for a further 2 minutes.

3 Add the lamb and cook for 6-8 minutes until colored, stirring constantly. Stir in the lentils, tomatoes, salt and black pepper. Pour over 2½ cups cold water and bring to a boil. Lower the heat, cover the pot and simmer for 1 hour. Remove the lid from the pot and continue to cook, uncovered, for a further 30 minutes, stirring occasionally, until the lamb is tender and the sauce is thick.

4 Taste and adjust the seasoning. Remove from the heat and serve immediately.

Plantation Stew

Stuffed Rolled Plantains
Piononos

This Puerto Rican dish is traditionally served with Rice 'n' Peas (see page 80).

2 tablespoons butter
⅔ cup oil plus 1 tablespoon
3 ripe plantains, peeled and cut in 4 long strips
2 eggs, lightly beaten

For the filling
1 tablespoon olive oil
1 small onion, minced
1 garlic clove, crushed
1lb ground beef
½ cup minced ham
2 tomatoes, peeled and diced
½ green pepper, seeded and finely chopped
6 olives, pitted and finely chopped
1 tablespoon capers, rinsed and finely chopped
1 tablespoon golden raisins, finely chopped
salt and freshly ground black pepper

Serves 6

1 Heat the butter and the 1 tablespoon oil together in a skillet over medium heat. Add the sliced plantains and cook, a few at a time, for 3-5 minutes until golden brown, turning once. Using a slotted spoon, transfer to paper towels. Curve into rings, securing with wooden cocktail picks.

2 Make the filling: Heat the oil in a skillet, add the onion and cook for 5 minutes over medium heat. Stir in garlic and ground beef. Cook for 5-10 minutes.

3 Add remaining filling ingredients, and season. Cook for a further 10 minutes, stirring frequently.

4 Fill each plantain ring with equal amounts of the meat mixture, smoothing the top of each ring flat.

5 Put the beaten eggs into a shallow bowl and dip each ring into the egg, coating all sides.

6 Heat the remaining oil in a heavy-bottomed skillet and cook the plantain rings, a few at a time, for 2-3 minutes until golden brown. Using a slotted spoon, transfer the rings to paper towels to drain.

7 Place on a warmed dish and serve at once.

Goat Water

A simple stew from Montserrat, Goat Water should be served with plain cooked rice and steamed dasheen or spinach leaves. Goat meat is similar to lamb, though it is much maligned, being thought of as tough and inedible. The meat of young kid (labeled chevon) is wonderfully delicate and can be favorably compared to baby lamb.

2 tablespoons oil
2 Bermuda onions, chopped
2 garlic cloves, crushed
2¼lb chevon (kid), cut in 1 inch cubes
2 tablespoons tomato paste
4 whole cloves
1 bay leaf
1 teaspoon salt
freshly ground black pepper
1 tablespoon soft butter
1 tablespoon all-purpose flour

Serves 4-6

1 Heat the oil in a large Dutch oven, add the onions and sauté for 6-8 minutes over medium heat until soft and golden, stirring frequently.

2 Add the garlic and kid and cook for 10 minutes until lightly browned.

3 Stir in the tomato paste and pour in 4 cups water. Add the cloves, bay leaf, salt and black pepper and bring to a boil. Boil for 10 minutes, skimming the foam that rises to the surface. Lower the heat, cover the pot and simmer for 2¼ hours, stirring occasionally.

4 Mix the butter and the flour together in a small bowl to a smooth paste. Stir the paste into the stew and cook, stirring constantly, for 2 minutes, until the sauce has thickened. Taste and adjust the seasoning and serve immediately.

Kidney Stew
Cocido de Rinones

Kidney Stew (Cocido de Rinones) reflects the Spanish influence in Caribbean cooking.

8 lamb kidneys, skinned and excess fat removed
1½ teaspoons salt
2 tablespoons all-purpose flour
freshly ground black pepper
¼ teaspoon curry powder
2 tablespoons oil
1 tablespoon minced fresh cilantro, for garnish

For the sauce
2 tablespoons oil
1 large Bermuda onion, minced
3 garlic cloves, crushed
4 bacon slices, diced
1 cup small button mushrooms, wiped clean and trimmed
2 tablespoons minced fresh cilantro
1¼ cups chicken stock
¼ cup rum
¼ cup fresh fresh orange juice

Serves 4

1 Slice the kidneys in half lengthwise and place in a bowl. Pour over enough cold water to cover and add 1 teaspoon of salt. Let soak for 10 minutes. Drain, then pat dry with paper towels.

2 Make the sauce: Heat the oil in a medium saucepan. Add the onion and sauté over medium heat for 6 minutes, or until soft and golden.

3 Stir in the garlic and bacon and cook for 5 minutes. Then add the mushrooms and cilantro and cook for 3 minutes. Pour over stock and bring to a boil. Lower heat and simmer for 15 minutes.

4 Meanwhile, mix the flour, ½ teaspoon salt, black pepper and curry powder together in a bowl. Toss the kidneys in the seasoned flour.

5 Heat the oil in a skillet and sauté kidneys over medium heat for 5 minutes, stirring constantly.

6 Add the kidneys to the sauce, pour over the rum and orange juice, and cook for a further 5 minutes. Serve, garnished with the fresh cilantro.

Mixed Meat Salad
Salpicon

Mixed Meat Salad or Salpicon is a well-known Cuban dish. This simple salad looks quite impressive when assembled and makes a colorful dish for a buffet.

½lb cold roast beef, diced
½lb cold roast chicken, diced
½lb cold honey roast ham, diced
1lb new potatoes, scrubbed, boiled and sliced
1 can (6oz) pineapple cubes, drained
1 sweet red pepper, seeded and diced
3 large gherkins, diced
4 scallions, trimmed and minced
4 celery stalks, diced
2 tablespoons minced fresh parsley
½ head iceberg lettuce, finely shredded
½ sweet red pepper, seeded and thinly sliced, for garnish

For the dressing
1 teaspoon sugar
1 teaspoon prepared mustard
pinch of cayenne
3 tablespoons white wine vinegar
½ cup olive oil
salt and freshly ground black pepper

Serves 6

1 Make the dressing: Mix the sugar, mustard and cayenne together in a bowl. Add the vinegar then gradually beat in the oil. Season to taste with salt and pepper.

2 In a large bowl, mix together the beef, chicken, ham, potatoes, pineapple, sweet red pepper, gherkins, scallions, celery and parsley. Pour over the dressing and toss the ingredients, ensuring they are completely coated.

3 Cover a large platter with the shredded lettuce.

4 Spoon the dressed salad onto the platter, building it into a mound. Garnish with the sliced sweet red pepper and serve immediately.

VEGETABLE DISHES AND RELISHES

Vegetables play an important role in the planning of Caribbean meals. West Indians love their staple vegetables and there are usually at least two starchy vegetable accompaniments to each main dish. Through the imaginative use of herbs and seasoning many of the rather bland starchy vegetables are transformed into exciting and tasty dishes in their own right. Curried Green Bananas (see page 81) and Yam Salad (see page 89) are just two examples. Today many of these West Indian vegetables are available in our own local markets. Try substituting sweet potatoes for ordinary potatoes, or chayote for squash or zucchini, or perhaps serve nutty-flavored Tannia Fritters (see page 74) as an extra vegetable accompaniment to steak.

Stuffed Pumpkin with Cashews

Stuffed Pumpkin with Cashews is an ideal dish to serve at a vegetarian dinner party. The pumpkin acts as an edible casserole and will keep the stuffing warm once it has been taken out of the oven for up to half an hour.

3½lb whole pumpkin

For the filling
¼ cup butter
1 large Bermuda onion, minced
4 scallions, trimmed and chopped
1 fresh chili, seeded and chopped
3 cups cashews, toasted
2 cups soft white bread crumbs
1 egg, lightly beaten
1 teaspoon salt
freshly ground black pepper
1 cup Cheddar cheese, shredded

Serves 6-8

1 Cut off 2 inches from the top of the pumpkin in a zig-zag line and reserve for the lid. Scoop out the seeds and membrane with a spoon and discard.

2 Preheat the oven to 350°F.

3 Make the filling: Heat 2 tablespoons of the butter in a large saucepan, add the onion and cook for 5 minutes. Stir in the scallions and chili and cook for a further 2 minutes, stirring frequently.

4 Stir in the cashews, bread crumbs, egg, salt, black pepper and Cheddar cheese.

5 Remove the pan from the heat and spoon the mixture into the pumpkin shell. Dot with the remaining butter, cover with the top of the pumpkin, place on a baking sheet and bake in the center of the oven for 1½ hours.

6 Remove from the oven and transfer to a serving dish. Serve cut in wedges.

Stuffed Pumpkin with Cashews

Spinach and Okra Purée
Vegetable Callaloo

In the Caribbean this is often called a Vegetable Callaloo – Spinach and Okra Purée is made in the same way as the soup Callaloo (see page 14), but without the crab and just a little stock.

1 tablespoon olive oil
1 large onion, minced
2 garlic cloves, crushed
½lb okra, trimmed and chopped
2 packages (10oz size) frozen spinach, thawed
⅓ cup chicken stock
⅞ cup coconut milk (see page 16)
1 teaspoon salt
freshly ground black pepper
dash of Trinidad Pepper Sauce (see page 95)

Serves 6-8

1 Heat the oil in a saucepan, add the onion and cook over medium heat for 5 minutes. Stir in the garlic and okra and cook, stirring frequently, for 3 minutes.

2 Add the spinach and pour in the stock, coconut milk, salt, pepper and a dash of pepper sauce.

3 Bring to a boil, lower the heat, cover the pan and simmer for 20 minutes.

4 Taste and adjust the seasoning. Transfer to a warmed serving dish and serve immediately.

Ackee and Cheese Soufflé

An unusual and elegant dish, Ackee and Cheese Soufflé can be served either as an appetizer or as part of a vegetarian meal.

3½ tablespoons butter
¼ cup all-purpose flour
⅞ cup milk
5 eggs, separated
¾ cup shredded Gruyère cheese
1 teaspoon salt
freshly ground black pepper
1 teaspoon Worcestershire sauce
¼ teaspoon prepared mustard
1 can (12oz) ackees, drained and mashed to a purée

Serves 4-6

1 Preheat the oven to 350°F.

2 Using ½ tablespoon of the butter, lightly grease a 7-cup soufflé dish.

3 Melt 3 tablespoons butter in a saucepan, sprinkle in the flour and stir over low heat for 2 minutes. Off heat, gradually stir in the milk. Return the pan to the heat, bring to a boil, lower the heat and simmer, stirring constantly for 2-3 minutes. Remove from the heat and let cool slightly before adding the egg yolks, one at a time, beating the mixture well.

4 Add the cheese, salt and pepper, Worcestershire and mustard, then stir in the ackee purée.

5 Using a hand-held electric mixer, beat the egg whites to stiff peaks, then fold carefully into the ackee mixture with a metal spoon. Pour the mixture into the prepared soufflé dish and bake in the oven for 30-35 minutes, until risen and lightly browned.

6 Remove from the oven and serve immediately.

Baked Chayotes au Gratin

A delicate French Creole dish from Martinique, flavored with a hint of nutmeg. Chayote, also known locally as cho-cho and christophene, is a tropical squash the size and shape of a pear.

4 chayotes
salt
5 tablespoons soft white bread crumbs

For the sauce
2 tablespoons butter
1 tablespoon all-purpose flour
1¼ cups milk
⅛ teaspoon grated nutmeg
½ teaspoon salt
freshly ground black pepper

Serves 4

1 Put the unpeeled chayotes in a large saucepan. Cover with water, add salt and bring to a boil. Cook for 25-30 minutes, or until tender when pierced with a knife. Drain and refresh under cold water.

2 When cool enough to handle, peel, quarter and cut out the seeds. Chop the flesh roughly then put in a blender or food processor and work for 30 seconds, to a rough purée. Pour the purée into a clean unbleached muslin cloth and squeeze tightly to drain off the excess liquid. Set aside.

3 Preheat the oven to 400°F.

4 Make the sauce: Melt the butter in a saucepan, sprinkle in the flour and cook over low heat, stirring constantly, for 2 minutes. Off heat, gradually stir in the milk. Season with the nutmeg, salt and pepper.

5 Return the pan to the heat and bring to a boil. Lower the heat and simmer, stirring constantly, for 3-5 minutes, until the sauce is thick enough to coat the back of the spoon.

6 Remove the pan from the heat and stir in the chayote purée.

7 Spoon the mixture into a shallow ovenproof dish, sprinkle over the bread crumbs and bake in the oven for 30 minutes.

Plantains Baked in Cheese Sauce

The riper the plantains the sweeter the taste. Plantains Baked in Cheese Sauce is a good dish to serve as part of a vegetarian meal or as a substantial vegetable accompaniment to barbecued meat.

3 tablespoons oil
3lb ripe plantains, peeled and sliced lengthwise

For the sauce
¼ cup butter
¼ cup all-purpose flour
2½ cups milk
1 bay leaf
¼ teaspoon grated nutmeg
1 teaspoon salt
freshly ground black pepper
2 cups shredded Cheddar cheese

Serves 6-8

1 Heat the oil in a large skillet. When the oil is hot, add the plantains, a few at a time, and cook for 1 minute until golden brown. Remove with a slotted spoon and transfer to paper towels to drain while cooking the remaining plantains.

2 Preheat the oven to 325°F.

3 Make the sauce: Melt the butter in a saucepan, sprinkle in the flour and cook, stirring constantly for 2 minutes. Off heat, gradually stir in the milk. Add the bay leaf and season with the nutmeg, salt and black pepper.

4 Return the pan to the heat, stir in half the cheese and bring to a boil. Lower the heat and simmer, stirring constantly, for 3-5 minutes or until the sauce is thick enough to coat the back of the spoon. Remove the pan from the heat and set aside.

5 Place a layer of plantain in the bottom of an ovenproof dish, pour over half the sauce and sprinkle over half the shredded cheese. Repeat with the remaining plantain and sauce, ending with a layer of shredded cheese.

6 Bake in the center of the oven for 1 hour; a lot of the sauce will have been absorbed into the plantains by this time.

7 Remove and serve immediately, from the dish.

Tannia Fritters

Tannia Fritters have a very distinctive slightly nutty flavor. The tannias are simply grated, seasoned, then deep-fried. Serve while they are still hot with drinks or as a vegetable accompaniment to Chicken Fricassée (see page 53).

2¼lb tannias
1 teaspoon salt
⅛ teaspoon grated nutmeg
freshly ground black pepper
¾ cup oil

Makes 24

1 Immerse the tannias in a saucepan of boiling water. Add the salt and continue boiling for 15 minutes. Drain and when cool enough to handle, peel and grate into a mixing bowl.

2 Season the grated tannia with the nutmeg, salt and black pepper and mix well together.

3 Heat the oil in a heavy-bottomed skillet. When the oil is hot, add tablespoons of the tannia mixture to the skillet, a few at a time, and cook for 2-3 minutes or until they are golden brown.

4 Remove with a slotted spoon and drain on paper towels. Keep warm while cooking the remaining fritters.

5 Transfer to a warmed serving dish and serve the fritters immediately.

Plantains Baked in Cheese Sauce (left) and Tannia Fritters

Breadfruit Oiled-down

This dish is usually made with salt meat or salt fish, sometimes both. The term "oiled-down" refers to a dish that has been cooked with coconut milk until all the liquid has been absorbed, leaving a small amount of coconut oil in the base of the pan.

½lb smoked ham, diced
1 tablespoon oil
1 large onion, minced
6 scallions, trimmed and minced
1 teaspoon dried thyme
4 cups coconut milk (see page 16)
3½lb whole breadfruit, quartered and peeled
1 teaspoon salt
1 hot seasoning pepper (optional)

Serves 6-8

1 Put the ham into a saucepan, cover with cold water and bring to a boil over medium heat. Skim the foam that rises to the surface. Lower the heat, cover the pan and simmer for 20-30 minutes until tender. Drain and set aside.

2 Heat the oil in a large saucepan, add the onion, scallions and thyme and cook for 5 minutes over medium heat, stirring frequently.

3 Pour over the coconut milk and bring to a boil. Lower the heat, add the ham, breadfruit, salt, black pepper and seasoning pepper, if using. Cover the pan and simmer for 30 minutes, or until the breadfruit is tender and the coconut milk has been absorbed, leaving only a thin film of coconut oil in the base of the pan.

4 Remove the seasoning pepper. Taste and adjust the seasoning, transfer to a warmed serving dish and serve immediately.

Candied Sweet Potatoes

The combination of orange juice, rum and sugar makes this dish something really special. For an attractive variation try combining white and orange sweet potatoes.

2¼lb sweet potatoes
4 tablespoons butter
3 tablespoons dark brown sugar
¾ cup fresh orange juice
2 tablespoons rum
⅛ teaspoon grated nutmeg

Serves 4-6

1 Put the unpeeled sweet potatoes in a large saucepan. Cover with cold water and bring to a boil over medium heat. Boil for 20 minutes or until just tender. Drain and when cool enough to handle, peel and cut the sweet potatoes into slices about ½ inch thick.

2 Preheat the oven to 350°F.

3 Using 1 tablespoon of the butter, grease a large shallow ovenproof serving dish. Arrange the sliced sweet potatoes in the dish. Dot with the remaining butter and sprinkle over the sugar.

4 Pour over the orange juice and rum. Sprinkle over the grated nutmeg and bake in the oven for 30 minutes.

5 Remove from the oven and serve immediately.

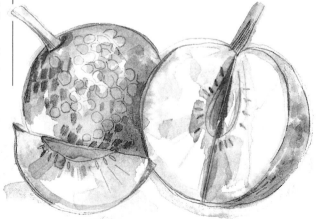

Bread fruit

Sautéed Topi Tambo

Topi tambo are root vegetables said to have been discovered in the Caribbean by the French colonists, who named them topin ambour. They are difficult to find outside the tropics but Jerusalem artichokes make a very good substitute.

1lb even-size topi tambo or Jerusalem artichokes,
washed, scrubbed and drained
salt and freshly ground black pepper
2 tablespoons butter
1 tablespoon olive oil
2 garlic cloves, crushed
grated rind and juice of 2 lemons
2 tablespoons minced fresh parsley
parsley sprigs, for garnish

Serves 4-6

1 Put the topi tambo or Jerusalem artichokes in a saucepan. Pour over enough cold water to cover. Add 1 teaspoon salt and bring to a boil over medium heat. Boil for 8 minutes, remove from the heat and drain. Set aside.

2 Heat the butter and oil together in a large skillet over medium heat. Add the garlic and cook for 1 minute.

3 Add the topi tambo or Jerusalem artichokes and sauté, stirring constantly for 5 minutes. Stir in the lemon rind and juice and the parsley. Season to taste with salt and black pepper.

4 Transfer to a warmed serving dish, garnish with parsley sprigs and serve immediately.

Eggplants in Coconut Sauce

Canned coconut milk is particularly good for this dish, which is simple to make and a great favorite with anyone who likes eggplants.

½lb eggplants
1 tablespoon salt
⅓ cup oil
2 tablespoons shredded coconut

For the sauce
2 tablespoons oil
2 onions, sliced
2 garlic cloves, crushed
6 tomatoes, peeled and chopped
1¼ cups coconut milk (see page 16)
salt and freshly ground black pepper

Serves 6

1 Cut the eggplants in ½ inch slices and place in a colander. Sprinkle with 1 tablespoon salt and leave to drain for 30 minutes. Rinse under cold water, then pat dry on paper towels.

2 Heat 2 tablespoons of the oil in a large skillet, add one third of the eggplants and cook for 10 minutes, turning once. Remove with a slotted spoon and drain on paper towels. Continue cooking the remaining eggplants in two batches, using 2 tablespoons of oil for each batch.

3 Preheat the oven to 350°F.

4 Make the sauce: Heat the oil, add the onions and sauté for 5 minutes over medium heat, until soft and golden. Add the garlic and tomatoes and cook for 3 minutes, stirring constantly.

5 Pour in the coconut milk, season to taste with salt and black pepper and bring to a boil. Lower the heat and simmer the sauce for 5 minutes.

6 Layer the eggplants in an ovenproof dish and pour over the coconut sauce. Cover with foil and bake in the oven for 30 minutes.

7 Remove from the oven, sprinkle over the shredded coconut then return to the oven and bake, uncovered, for a further 5-10 minutes, until the coconut is golden brown.

Black Beans and Rice
Moros y Cristianos

A Cuban specialty, this dish is called Moros Y Cristianos (Moors and Christians) in Spanish referring to the black and white color of the dish. Black beans have a strong almost meaty flavor and are used a great deal in Cuban cooking.

1½ cups dried black beans
½lb smoked ham, trimmed of fat
and skin, then diced
2 tablespoons olive oil
1 onion, minced
2 garlic cloves, crushed
2 tomatoes, peeled and chopped
1 green pepper, seeded and finely chopped
1¼ cups long-grain white rice, rinsed and drained
salt and freshly ground black pepper

Serves 6

1 Put the beans in a colander and pour over boiling water. Transfer to a large saucepan, add the diced ham and cover with cold water. Bring to a boil over medium heat and cook for 10 minutes, skimming off any foam. Lower heat, cover pan and simmer for 45-60 minutes, until beans are tender. Remove from heat and drain. Set meat to one side and refresh beans under cold water.

2 Heat the oil in a large saucepan, add the onion and sauté for 5 minutes. Add garlic, tomatoes and green pepper and cook for 5 minutes, stirring.

3 Add the rice, beans and ham to the pan and season to taste. Pour in 2½ cups of cold water and bring to a boil over medium heat. Lower heat, cover pan and simmer for 20 minutes, until the rice is tender and the liquid has been absorbed.

4 Taste and adjust the seasoning. Transfer to a warmed serving dish and serve at once.

Creole Ratatouille

Serve as the ideal accompaniment to roast meat.

2 tablespoons olive oil
1 large onion, finely sliced
2 scallions, trimmed and chopped
2 garlic cloves, crushed
1 fresh chili, seeded and minced
1 eggplant, peeled and cut in 1 inch cubes
1 sweet red pepper, seeded and cut in 1 inch cubes
¼lb okra, trimmed and chopped
2 celery stalks, trimmed and chopped
1 chayote, peeled, seeded and chopped
1 can (16 oz) tomatoes, drained and chopped
1 teaspoon dried thyme
1 teaspoon minced fresh basil
½ teaspoon brown sugar
salt and freshly ground black pepper
basil leaves, for garnish

Serves 4-6

1 Heat the oil in a Dutch oven. Add the onion, scallions and garlic and cook over low heat for 6 minutes, stirring constantly.

2 Stir in the chili, eggplant, sweet red pepper, okra, celery, chayote, tomatoes, thyme, basil and sugar. Season to taste with salt and black pepper. Pour in 2 cups cold water and bring to a boil over medium heat. Lower the heat, cover the pot and simmer for 45-60 minutes, stirring pot occasionally and adding more water if necessary.

3 Taste and adjust the seasoning, then garnish with basil. Serve hot or cold.

Creole Ratatouille (front) and Black Beans and Rice

Creamed Eddoes

Eddoe, also known as taro, dasheen or "old cocoyam", is a root vegetable belonging to the Arum family. The leaves are called dasheen or callaloo and are used to make the well-known soup of the same name.

1lb eddoes
2 tablespoons butter
4 scallions, trimmed and minced
2 teaspoons fresh lime juice
1 cup milk
¼ teaspoon Trinidad Pepper Sauce (see page 95)
salt and white pepper

Serves 4

1 Put the unpeeled eddoes in a saucepan. Cover with cold water and bring to a boil over medium heat. Lower the heat, cover the pan and simmer for 20-30 minutes until tender. Drain and when cool enough to handle, peel off the skins.

2 Meanwhile, heat the butter in a saucepan, add the scallions and cook for 3 minutes, stirring constantly over medium heat until soft and golden.

3 Off heat, stir in the lime juice. Add the eddoes and the milk and mash to a purée with a potato masher.

4 Season the purée with the pepper sauce, salt and white pepper and spoon into a warmed serving dish. Serve immediately.

Rice 'n' Peas

Rice 'n' Peas is another inter-island specialty but is generally associated with Jamaica, where it is traditionally served for Sunday lunch. The dish is in fact usually made with red kidney beans which are called "peas" in Jamaica, but can be made with fresh gungo (pigeon) peas.

¾ cup dried red kidney beans, soaked in cold water for
2 hours or overnight and drained
4 cups coconut milk (see page 16)
1 sprig fresh thyme
1 hot seasoning pepper
4 scallions, trimmed and minced
2 garlic cloves, crushed
1 teaspoon salt
freshly ground black pepper
2½ cups long-grain white rice

Serves 6-8

1 Put the beans in a colander and scald with boiling water. Transfer to a large saucepan and pour in the coconut milk. Bring to a boil over medium heat. Lower the heat, cover the pan and simmer for 45 minutes, until tender.

2 Add the thyme, seasoning pepper, scallions, garlic, salt and black pepper.

3 Wash the rice, drain and add to the beans. Add 1¼ cups cold water and bring to a boil over medium heat. Lower the heat, cover the pan and simmer for 20 minutes, or until the rice is tender and all the liquid has been absorbed.

4 Remove the seasoning pepper and mix the rice and beans together with a fork. Transfer to a warmed serving dish and serve immediately.

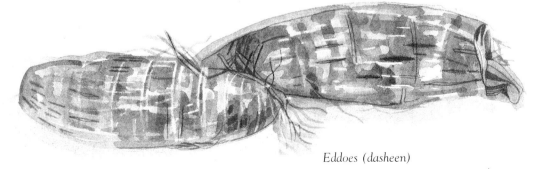

Eddoes (dasheen)

Creole Rice

The hot seasoning pepper gives Creole Rice a characteristic Caribbean flavor.

2 tablespoons olive oil
1 onion, minced
2 garlic cloves, crushed
1¼ cups rice, rinsed and drained
1 hot seasoning pepper
salt and freshly ground black pepper
2 tablespoons minced fresh parsley
1 sweet red pepper, seeded and finely sliced

Serves 4

1 Heat the oil in a saucepan over medium heat. Add the onion and cook for 5 minutes. Lower the heat, add the garlic and cook for 1 minute.

2 Stir in the rice and cook for 1 minute. Pour in 2½ cups boiling water, and add the seasoning pepper. Cover the pan and cook for 15-20 minutes, until the rice is tender and the water is absorbed.

3 Remove the seasoning pepper and season to taste with salt and black pepper.

4 Transfer to a warmed serving dish. Sprinkle over the parsley and the sliced red pepper and serve the rice immediately.

Curried Green Bananas

Curried Green Bananas will add spice to any meal. Serve as a vegetable accompaniment to any of these Caribbean dishes or as part of an Indian meal. If a sweeter flavor is preferred use slightly riper bananas and reduce the cooking time.

2 tablespoons oil
1 onion, finely sliced
1 tablespoon garam masala
4 green bananas, peeled and cut in 1 inch slices
1¾ cups coconut milk (see page 16)
salt and freshly ground black pepper
1 tablespoon minced fresh cilantro, for garnish

Serves 4

1 Heat the oil in a saucepan, add the onion and sauté over medium heat for 6 minutes.

2 Add the garam masala to the pan and cook, stirring constantly for 1 minute.

3 Add the green bananas and cook for a further 5 minutes, until lightly browned.

4 Pour over the coconut milk. Season to taste with salt and black pepper and bring to a boil. Lower the heat, cover the pan and simmer for 30 minutes.

5 Transfer to a warmed serving dish, garnish with the chopped cilantro and serve immediately.

Stuffed Sweet Potato Balls

These unusual potato balls are so delicious they could be eaten just by themselves. They are crisp on the outside with a center filling of sweet potato, melted cheese and olives.

2¼lb sweet potatoes, peeled and cubed
2 teaspoons salt
¼ cup butter
2 eggs, beaten
freshly ground black pepper
¼ cup Mozzarella or Edam cheese, cut in 18 cubes
18 stuffed olives
1½ cups dry bread crumbs
oil, for deep-frying
parsley sprigs, for garnish

Makes 18

1 Put the sweet potatoes into a large saucepan. Pour over enough cold water to cover. Add 1 teaspoon of the salt and bring to a boil over medium heat. Cover and cook for 15 minutes, until soft.

2 Remove from the heat, drain and return to the pan. Add the butter, the remaining salt, half the beaten egg and black pepper to taste. Using a potato masher, mash to a smooth purée.

3 Form the purée into eighteen 2 inch balls. Push a piece of cheese and an olive into the center of each ball and re-form the potato around them.

4 Sprinkle the bread crumbs onto one large plate, and pour the remaining beaten egg into a bowl. Roll the potato balls, first in the egg then in the bread crumbs until well coated.

5 Heat about 3 inches of oil in a saucepan. When hot, add the potato balls and cook, a few at a time, for 2-2½ minutes until golden brown. Using a slotted spoon transfer the fried potato balls to paper towels to drain. Keep warm while cooking the remaining potato balls.

7 Transfer to a warmed serving dish, garnish with the parsley sprigs and serve immediately.

Okra in Spicy Tomato Sauce

A delicious dish for those who enjoy garlic and chili.

1lb okra, trimmed

For the sauce
2 tablespoons olive oil
1 large Bermuda onion, minced
4 garlic cloves, crushed
6 large tomatoes, peeled and chopped
1 fresh chili, minced
1 tablespoon minced fresh basil
⅛ teaspoon curry powder
1 teaspoon salt
freshly ground black pepper
basil leaves, for garnish

Serves 4

1 Make the sauce: Heat the oil in a large saucepan. Add the onion and sauté over medium heat for 5 minutes until soft and golden.

2 Add the garlic and cook for a further 2 minutes, stirring constantly.

3 Stir in the tomatoes, chili, basil, curry powder, salt and pepper, and pour over ¾ cup water. Bring to a boil, then reduce the heat and simmer for 5 minutes.

4 Add the prepared okra to the pan and cook for 15-20 minutes, depending on the size of the okra, stirring occasionally.

5 Taste and adjust the seasoning. Transfer to a warmed serving dish, garnish with basil leaves and serve immediately.

Okra in Spicy Tomato Sauce (front) and
Stuffed Sweet Potato Balls

Black-Eyed Pea Fritters
Akkra

Black-Eyed Pea Fritters, which originally came from West Africa, are found throughout the Caribbean. In Jamaica they are called Akkra and in the Dutch islands, Calas.

1¼ cups dried black-eyed peas
1 green pepper, seeded and finely chopped
½ teaspoon Trinidad Pepper Sauce (see page 95)
salt and freshly ground black pepper
1 cup oil

Makes 36

1 Put the peas in a bowl and pour over boiling water to cover. Let soak overnight. Drain and refresh under cold water then rub the skins off the peas with your fingers or between a dish towel.

2 Put the skinned peas and the chopped pepper into a blender or food processor and work to a smooth purée, adding a little water if necessary. Alternatively pound in a mortar.

3 Add the pepper sauce to the purée and season to taste with salt and black pepper.

4 Heat the oil in a heavy-bottomed skillet. Drop tablespoons of the purée, a few at a time, into the oil and cook for 2-3 minutes, until golden brown, turning once. Remove with a slotted spoon and transfer to paper towels to drain while making the remaining fritters.

5 Arrange the fritters on a warmed serving dish and serve immediately.

Plantain Balls
Foo Foo

Serve these pounded green Plantain Balls, or Foo Foo, with soups or stews as a rather unusual substitute for dumplings.

2 green plantains
salt and freshly ground black pepper

Makes 12

1 Put the unpeeled plantains into a large saucepan. Pour in enough cold water to cover and bring to a boil over medium heat. Lower the heat and simmer the plantains for 30 minutes until soft and the skins have begun to split.

2 Drain the plantains and when cool enough to handle, peel and place in a mortar. Season to taste with salt and black pepper.

3 Pound the plantains with a pestle for 25-30 minutes or until they form a smooth ball, dipping the pestle into cold water from time to time to prevent it from sticking.

4 Wetting your hands, roll the plantains into small balls and add to soups or stews as a garnish.

Cornmeal and Okra Pudding
Coo Coo

Cornmeal and Okra Pudding is found throughout the Caribbean. In Barbados it is called Coo Coo, in the Dutch and Virgin islands it is called Fungi or Funchi. It is served as a starchy vegetable to accompany either meat or fish.

6oz okra, trimmed and sliced
1½ teaspoons salt
2 cups coarse cornmeal
¼ cup butter

For the garnish
½ sweet red pepper, seeded and diced
½ green pepper, seeded and diced

Serves 6-8

1 Put the okra into a medium saucepan. Add 4 cups cold water and the salt and bring to a boil over medium heat. Lower the heat, cover the pan and simmer for 10 minutes.

2 Using a wooden spoon, gradually stir in the cornmeal a little at a time. Continue cooking, stirring constantly, for 5 minutes, until the mixture comes away from the side and base of the pan and forms a solid ball.

3 Using half the butter, grease a round serving dish. Spoon in the cornmeal, smoothing the top flat. Spread the remaining butter over the top.

4 Garnish with the diced peppers and serve at once.

Corn Pie

A good family dish, Corn Pie is the perfect accompaniment to the tasty Pineapple Spare Ribs (see page 61).

2 tablespoons oil
1 onion, minced
2 cans (11oz each) cream-style corn
2 eggs, beaten
2 teaspoons Worcestershire sauce
⅛ teaspoon paprika
salt and freshly ground black pepper

Serves 4

1 Preheat the oven to 350°F.

2 Heat the oil in a small skillet. Add the onion and sauté over medium heat for 5 minutes.

3 Transfer the onion to an ovenproof serving dish. Stir in the corn, eggs, Worcestershire and paprika. Season to taste with salt and black pepper.

4 Bake in the oven for 45 minutes until firm and golden brown on the top. Serve immediately.

Sunshine Salad

Serve this attractive bitter-sweet salad as part of a buffet meal or as a refreshing accompaniment to most poultry or meat dishes.

4 oranges, peeled and sliced
2 large firm ripe mangoes, peeled and sliced
3 large heads of Belgian endive, washed, dried
and leaves separated
1 tablespoon minced fresh chives, for garnish

For the dressing
1 teaspoon prepared mustard
1 teaspoon sugar
2 garlic cloves, crushed
2 tablespoons minced fresh chives
½ teaspoon grated orange rind
2 tablespoons fresh orange juice
2 tablespoons fresh lime juice
⅓ cup olive oil
salt and freshly ground black pepper

Serves 4-6

1 Make the dressing: Mix the mustard, sugar, garlic and chives together in a mixing bowl. Stir in the orange rind, orange juice and lime juice and gradually beat in the oil. Season to taste with salt and freshly ground black pepper.

2 Arrange the oranges, mangoes and endive on a plate in the shape of a sunburst. Pour over the dressing, sprinkle with the chives, and serve immediately.

Bean Salad

Bean Salad improves with keeping and should be made at least one day before you wish to serve it.

⅔ cup dried red kidney beans, soaked overnight
and drained
⅔ cup dried cannellini beans, soaked overnight
and drained
1 large onion, thinly sliced
2 scallions, trimmed and minced
1 cup cauliflower flowerets
2 celery stalks, chopped
½ green pepper, seeded and thinly sliced
½ sweet red pepper, seeded and thinly sliced
3 tablespoons minced fresh parsley

For the dressing
2 teaspoons salt
⅓ cup packed dark brown sugar
⅔ cup malt vinegar

Serves 6

1 Put the drained beans in a large saucepan. Cover with cold water and bring to a boil over medium heat. Boil for 10 minutes, skimming off any foam that rises to the surface. Lower the heat and simmer for 1-1½ hours, or until the beans are tender. Drain, refresh under cold water and transfer to a large mixing bowl. Let cool.

2 Add the onion, scallions, cauliflower, celery, green and sweet red pepper and parsley to the beans.

3 Make the dressing: Put the salt, sugar, vinegar and ¼ cup of water into a small saucepan. Bring to a boil over medium heat and continue boiling for about 30 seconds. Remove from the heat and let cool.

4 Pour the cooled dressing over the vegetables and mix well. Cover with plastic wrap and refrigerate for at least 4 hours or overnight, stirring occasionally.

5 Transfer the salad to a serving bowl and serve at room temperature.

On previous page, clockwise from the left: Bean Salad, Tropical Spinach Salad, Sunshine Salad and Yam salad.

Tropical Spinach Salad

Use young tender spinach leaves for this salad. An interesting combination of spinach, papaya, bacon and cashews provides a delicate balance of sweet and savory flavors. Additional bacon can be used to make a slightly more substantial salad which can be served with crusty French bread as a light lunchtime meal.

6 slices bacon
¾lb fresh young spinach
1 papaya, peeled, quartered, seeded and thinly sliced
1 cup cashews, toasted

For the dressing
1 teaspoon prepared mustard
2 garlic cloves, crushed
3 tablespoons white wine vinegar
⅓ cup olive oil
salt and freshly ground black pepper

Serves 4-6

1 Make the dressing: Mix the mustard and garlic together in a mixing bowl. Stir in the vinegar and gradually beat in the oil. Season to taste with salt and black pepper.

2 Preheat the broiler to high and broil the bacon for 5-7 minutes on each side until crisp. Set aside to cool. When cool cut up into small pieces

3 Rinse the spinach under cold water and dry thoroughly. Pull the leaves from the stems. Discard the stems and place the leaves in a salad bowl. Add the papaya, nuts and bacon.

4 Just before serving pour over the dressing and toss the salad.

Yam Salad

One of the staple foods of the Caribbean, yam, when prepared in this way, makes an imaginative alternative to potato salad.

1½lb yam
2 dill pickles, finely chopped
2 hard-cooked eggs, chopped
2 tomatoes, diced
3 scallions, trimmed and minced
2 celery stalks, diced
1 tablespoon minced fresh chives
1 teaspoon salt
freshly ground black pepper
1 teaspoon paprika

For the dressing
½ cup mayonnaise
3 tablespoons plain yogurt
2 tablespoons distilled white vinegar

Serves 6-8

1 Make the dressing: Mix the mayonnaise, yogurt and vinegar together in a small bowl. Set aside.

2 Put the unpeeled yam in a large saucepan. Cover with water and bring to a boil. Cook for 20-25 minutes, until tender when tested with a knife.

3 Drain and when just cool enough to handle, peel and chop the yam into ½ inch cubes.

4 Put the warm yam into a large mixing bowl and pour over the dressing, mixing well to ensure the yam is thoroughly coated.

5 Add the pickles, eggs, tomatoes, scallions, celery, chives, salt, pepper and paprika and mix well.

6 Transfer to a serving bowl. Cover with plastic wrap and chill in the refrigerator for 1 hour. Mix well before serving.

Avocado and Pink Grapefruit Salad

Avocado and grapefruit are a favorite combination in the Caribbean where avocados, also called zabocas or alligator pears, can weigh up to several pounds each. They have smooth shiny skins and yellow buttery flesh.

2 pink grapefruit
2 large firm ripe avocados

For the dressing
1 teaspoon sugar
1 teaspoon Dijon mustard
1 large garlic clove, crushed
¼ cup fresh grapefruit juice
⅓ cup olive oil
salt and freshly ground black pepper

Serves 4

1 Make the dressing: Mix the sugar, mustard and garlic together in a bowl. Pour over the grapefruit juice and mix well. Gradually pour in the oil, beating the mixture with a wire whip. Season to taste with salt and pepper.

2 Peel the grapefruit and separate into sections, discarding the seeds and membrane.

3 Peel and thinly slice the avocados, lengthwise.

4 Arrange the avocados and grapefruit on a large round serving dish. Pour over the dressing and serve immediately.

Soused Green Bananas

Green bananas are used a great deal in West Indian cooking as a starchy vegetable. They are also known locally as green figs. Soused Green Bananas tastes even better if made a few days before serving.

5 green bananas
1 cucumber, thinly sliced

For the dressing
1 tablespoon salt
1 large onion, minced
juice of 2 limes
freshly ground black pepper

Serves 6-8

1 Put the unpeeled green bananas in a large saucepan, cover with cold water and bring to a boil over medium heat. Lower the heat and simmer for 30 minutes, or until the skins of the bananas split.

2 Drain and when cool enough to handle, peel and scrape the bananas and slice in 1 inch lengths.

3 Put the sliced bananas into a heatproof bowl. Pour over enough boiling water to cover. Add the salt, onion, lime juice and black pepper to taste.

4 When cool, cover the bowl with plastic wrap and refrigerate overnight.

5 Add the cucumber slices and serve immediately.

Avocado and Pink Grapefruit Salad (front) and
Soused Green Bananas

Caribbean Coleslaw

A sweet coleslaw which should be served with a salty meat such as ham or salt beef.

½ small white cabbage, finely shredded
4 large carrots, finely shredded
1 can (16oz) pineapple cubes, drained

For the dressing
¼ cup condensed milk
1 tablespoon prepared mustard
1 teaspoon salt
½ cup olive oil
¾ cup evaporated milk
3 tablespoons white wine vinegar
freshly ground black pepper

Serves 6

1 Make the mayonnaise: Mix the condensed milk, mustard and salt together in a bowl. Using a hand-held mixer gradually add the oil, a drop at a time, beating constantly until the mixture has thickened. Then continue to add the oil in a thin stream, beating constantly. Gradually beat in the evaporated milk, then the vinegar and black pepper. Taste and add more salt if necessary.

2 Mix the cabbage, carrot and pineapple cubes together in a large mixing bowl. Pour over the dressing and toss well, ensuring all the ingredients are thoroughly coated.

3 Transfer to a glass serving bowl. Cover with plastic wrap and chill in the refrigerator until ready to serve.

Carrot and Raisin Salad

The cinnamon in this salad gives it a distinctive and unusual flavor. A good tip for crisping carrots is to soak them in ice water for 1 hour before you shred them.

3 cups shredded carrots
⅔ cup golden raisins
juice of ½ orange
juice of ½ lime
¼ cup mayonnaise
1¼ teaspoons ground cinnamon
½ teaspoon salt
freshly ground black pepper

Serves 4

1 Put the carrots and golden raisins into a mixing bowl. Pour over the fresh orange and lime juice and mix gently but thoroughly.

2 Gradually stir in the mayonnaise. Add 1 teaspoon of the cinnamon, the salt and black pepper and mix well, ensuring that all the ingredients are evenly distributed in the bowl.

3 Spoon into a serving bowl, sprinkle over the remaining cinnamon and serve at once.

Rice and Pepper Salad with Tomato Dressing

This tangy rice salad flavored with tomatoes, peppers and garlic is delicious served with any meat, fish or poultry dish. It is very important to rinse the rice thoroughly before cooking to prevent it from becoming sticky.

2 tablespoons olive oil
1 onion, minced
2 garlic cloves, crushed
1 sweet red pepper, seeded and diced
1 green pepper, seeded and diced
1¼ cups rice, well rinsed and drained
1 hot seasoning pepper
salt and freshly ground black pepper

For the dressing
5 tomatoes, peeled, seeded and chopped
1 garlic clove
2 tablespoons red wine vinegar
⅓ cup olive oil
1 teaspoon dried thyme

For garnish
tomato slices
fresh thyme sprigs

Serves 4-6

1 Make the dressing: Put the chopped tomatoes, garlic, wine vinegar, olive oil, thyme and salt and pepper together in an electric blender or food processor and work for 30-60 seconds, or until it is smooth and fairly thick.

2 Heat the oil in a saucepan over medium heat. Add the onion and cook for 5 minutes until soft. Lower the heat, add the garlic, sweet red and green peppers and cook for 2 minutes.

3 Stir in the rice and cook for 1 minute. Pour in 2½ cups boiling water and add the seasoning pepper. Cover the pan and cook for 15-20 minutes, until the rice is tender and the water is absorbed.

4 Remove the seasoning pepper and season to taste with salt and pepper.

5 Transfer to a serving dish and pour over the tomato dressing. Mix well together and set aside to cool.

6 Garnish with the tomato slices and thyme sprigs before serving.

Cucumber and Coconut Salad

Spicy and refreshing, Cucumber and Coconut Salad reflects the East Indian influence that is present in Caribbean cooking.

1 cucumber, seeded and cut in ½ inch cubes
3 tablespoons shredded coconut

For the dressing
2 teaspoons sugar
¼ cup fresh lime or lemon juice
½ teaspoon seeded and minced fresh chili
salt and white pepper

Serves 4

1 Make the dressing: Mix the sugar with the lime or lemon juice in a small bowl. Add the chili, season with salt and white pepper to taste and mix well.

2 Put the cucumber into a serving bowl, pour over the dressing and mix well, ensuring the pieces are thoroughly coated. Sprinkle over the coconut and serve immediately.

Trinidad Pepper Sauce

Each island in the Caribbean has its own recipe for a hot pepper sauce. It is served as a condiment with most meals and when used with discretion can become quite addictive.

½lb red, green and yellow hot seasoning peppers, seeded and minced
2 large onions, minced
2 garlic cloves, minced
½ small unripe papaya, peeled, seeded and finely chopped
2 teaspoons Dijon mustard
½ teaspoon turmeric
1 teaspoon salt
2⅔ cups distilled white vinegar

Makes about 4 cups

1 Put the peppers, onions, garlic, papaya, mustard, turmeric, salt and vinegar into a saucepan. Bring to a boil over medium heat. Lower the heat and simmer for 5 minutes.

2 Pour into warmed sterilized jars, cover with a round of waxed paper and seal with airtight, vinegar-proof lids. The sauce will keep for several months.

Pepper Wine

A few drops of Pepper Wine transform a simple soup or stew into an exotic West Indian dish.

3 hot seasoning peppers
1 standard bottle dry sherry

1 Put the peppers into a large glass preserving jar, pour over the sherry and leave for 2 weeks. (Keep the sherry bottle.)

2 Using a funnel, pour the sherry back into the bottle, adding one of the peppers, and use as required.

From the left: Pepper Jelly, Sweet Pepper Sauce (on shelf) and Garlic and Pepper Sauce, Trinidad Pepper Sauce, Chow Chow, Pepper Wine

Sweet Pepper Sauce

Sweet Pepper Sauce is an adaptation of a traditional pepper and tomato sauce served with black beans in Cuba. Serve this spicy sauce with beans, meat, fish or rice.

¾ cup olive oil
1½lb tomatoes, peeled and chopped
1lb sweet red peppers, seeded and minced
1 bay leaf
1 fresh red chili, seeded and minced
3 garlic cloves, crushed
1 teaspoon dried oregano
1 tablespoon minced fresh cilantro
1 teaspoon sugar
salt and freshly ground black pepper
¼ cup white wine vinegar

Makes approximately 5 cups

1 Heat the oil in a saucepan, add the tomatoes, sweet red peppers and bay leaf and cook over medium heat for 10 minutes, stirring constantly.

2 Add the chili, garlic, oregano, cilantro and sugar. Season to taste with salt and black pepper. Lower the heat and cook for a further 15 minutes, stirring frequently, until the sauce is thick. Remove from the heat and pour in the vinegar.

3 Pour into warmed sterilized jars and seal with airtight vinegar-proof lids. The sauce will keep for several months.

Spicy Mustard Pickle
Chow Chow

Spicy Mustard Pickle will keep for several months in an airtight jar. Serve Chow Chow with cold cuts and salads.

½ small cauliflower, separated into small flowerets
2 green tomatoes, chopped
2 onions, chopped
3 carrots, chopped
10 green beans, trimmed and chopped
1 fresh chili, seeded and chopped
2 tablespoons salt
1½ cups white wine vinegar
2 tablespoons cornstarch
2 tablespoons sugar
1 tablespoon dry mustard
1 teaspoon curry powder
1 teaspoon turmeric

Makes about 5 cups

1 Put the cauliflower, tomatoes, onions, carrots, beans and chili in a large mixing bowl. Pour over 4 cups cold water and stir in the salt. Cover the bowl and leave overnight.

2 Drain the vegetables and transfer to a saucepan. Pour in 1¼ cups cold water, add 2 tablespoons of the vinegar and bring to a boil over medium heat. Lower the heat and simmer for 5 minutes.

3 Meanwhile mix the cornstarch, sugar, mustard, curry powder and turmeric together in a bowl. Stir in the remaining vinegar to form a smooth paste. Mix a little of the hot cooking water into the paste then pour the paste into the pan. Simmer for 2 minutes then remove from the heat.

4 Transfer to warmed sterilized jars and seal with screw-top vinegar-proof lids.

Garlic and Pepper Sauce

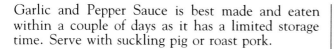

Garlic and Pepper Sauce is best made and eaten within a couple of days as it has a limited storage time. Serve with suckling pig or roast pork.

2 hot seasoning peppers, seeded and chopped
2 green peppers, seeded and chopped
6 garlic cloves
2 tablespoons minced fresh parsley
juice of 2 limes
½ cup olive oil
1 teaspoon salt
freshly ground black pepper

Makes 2 cups

1 Put the seasoning peppers, green peppers, garlic and parsley into a blender or food processor and work for 30 seconds to a smooth purée.

2 Pour in the lime juice, olive oil, salt and black pepper and work for a further 15 seconds until thoroughly blended. Pour into sterilized jars and seal with airtight lids. Store in the refrigerator for up to 1 week.

Pepper Jelly

Pepper Jelly is slightly hot and very sweet. It is delicious served with any roast meat.

6 cups chopped tart apples
⅔ cup distilled white vinegar
2 cups granulated sugar
2 hot seasoning peppers

Makes about 1½lb

1 Put the apples in a large heavy-bottomed saucepan along with the vinegar and 2 cups water. Bring to a boil, then lower the heat slightly and simmer for 20-25 minutes, or until the apples are very soft and pulpy.

2 Hang a jelly bag over a large bowl and pour the apple pulp into the bag. Let the pulp strain through overnight.

3 Transfer the strained juice to a large kettle, add the sugar and 1 seasoning pepper and heat gently, stirring constantly, until the sugar has dissolved. Bring to a boil, then continue to boil vigorously for about 5 minutes until a teaspoon of the jelly placed on a cold saucer wrinkles when a finger is pulled across the surface. Alternatively, use the sheeting test. Discard the seasoning pepper.

4 Remove the kettle from the heat and skim off any foam. Seed and finely chop the remaining seasoning pepper, then stir into the jelly. Pour the jelly immediately into warmed sterilized 1-cup jelly glasses, filling them to within ¼ inch of the tops. Seal with ⅛ inch melted paraffin. Cool, cover and store for up to 9 months.

DESSERTS

Caribbean desserts tend to be either very sweet, very fruity or very alcoholic, usually a mixture of all three. Because dairy products such as fresh cream are unavailable on most of the islands, those who live there have to rely on canned cream, evaporated and condensed milk. But the recipes in this section, where possible, have been adapted to use fresh cream. Coconut is also used a great deal as the basis for many of their delicious desserts. In my opinion though, it is the tropical fruits with their exotic flavors and colors (see Tropical Fruit Platter, page 105) that provide the best ending to any Caribbean meal.

Mango and Coconut Meringue

The best way to eat a mango is sitting in the bath! The second best way is to eat it in a dessert like Mango and Coconut Meringue. The meringue can be made the day before and should be filled just before serving.

4 egg whites
pinch of salt
1 cup superfine sugar
1 teaspoon cornstarch
1 teaspoon white wine vinegar
3 tablespoons shredded coconut
3 bay leaves, to decorate

For the filling
2 large firm ripe mangoes, peeled and sliced
2 cups heavy cream
2 tablespoons superfine sugar
1 egg white

Serves 6-8

1 Preheat the oven to 275°F.

2 Using a hand-held electric mixer, beat the egg whites with a pinch of salt to stiff peaks. Gradually beat in the superfine sugar, then continue beating for 5 minutes.

3 Fold the cornstarch, vinegar and coconut into the meringue mixture. Line a baking sheet with silicone paper. Using a slim spatula, shape the meringue in a 9 inch circle on the baking sheet, building up the edges to form a ridge.

4 Bake in the center of the oven for 10 minutes, then lower the oven temperature to 225°F and cook for a further 45 minutes. Switch off the oven and leave the meringue in the cooling oven for 1 hour. Remove and transfer to a large flat serving platter.

5 Make the filling: Put one of the sliced mangoes in a blender or food processor and process for 30 seconds to a smooth purée. Transfer to a bowl and set aside.

6 Using a hand-held electric mixer, gently whip the cream and sugar together until it is thick and firm. Beat the egg white in another bowl to stiff peaks, then fold into the cream with the mango purée.

7 Fill the center of the meringue with the cream and mango mixture. Decorate the top with the remaining mango slices and bay leaves and serve.

Coconut Meringue front and Lime Bombe
with Mango Sauce

Lime Bombe with Mango Sauce

Lime Bombe with Mango Sauce is an impressive dessert to serve at an elegant dinner party. If limes are unavailable lemons may be used instead.

finely grated rind of 3 limes
juice of 4 limes
3 eggs, separated
pinch of salt
½ cup superfine sugar
1¼ cups heavy cream

For the mango sauce
1 can (16 oz) mangoes
juice of 1 lime

To decorate
cubes of mango
shreds of lime rind

Serves 6-8

1 Mix the lime rind and juice together in a bowl.

2 Using a hand-held electric mixer, beat the egg whites with a pinch of salt to stiff peaks. Gradually beat in 6 tablespoons of the sugar. Beat the egg yolks into the mixture.

3 In a separate bowl, whip the cream with the remaining sugar, then add the mixed lime rind and juice and beat until firm.

4 Using a metal spoon, fold the lime mixture into the egg mixture. Pour into a 4-cup pudding mold, cover with plastic wrap and freeze overnight.

5 Make the sauce: Put the mangoes and their juice with the lime juice into a blender or food processor and work for 30 seconds to a smooth purée. Strain into a small pitcher.

6 Unmold the bombe 2 hours before serving: Dip the bottom of the bowl into a sink of cold water, run a knife around the inside edge and invert onto a serving platter. Return to the freezer.

7 About 15 minutes before serving, remove the bombe from the freezer and place in the refrigerator. Just before serving, decorate with mango and lime rind. Pour a little of the sauce over the top and pass the rest separately in the pitcher.

Coconut Mold

Coconut Mold can be made with shredded coconut instead of fresh (see page 16), and is a great favorite with children.

1 coconut
2½ cups milk
1½ tablespoons unflavored gelatin
3 tablespoons sugar
2 tablespoons golden raisins (optional)

Serves 4-6

1 Split open the coconut and remove the flesh. Cut away the brown skin and grate the flesh. Transfer to a bowl.

2 Bring the milk to just below the boiling point and pour over the grated coconut. Leave for 30 minutes, stirring frequently. Strain the milk into a saucepan, squeezing the coconut with your hands to extract all the liquid.

3 Mix the gelatin with 3 tablespoons of the coconut milk in a small ramekin, and pour the mixture into the saucepan.

4 Add the sugar, place the pan over low heat and cook for 3 minutes, stirring constantly. Do not allow to boil. Stir in the golden raisins, if using, and pour into a 2½ cup mold. Let cool.

5 When cool, place in the refrigerator for 2-3 hours until set.

6 Unmold and serve immediately.

Creole Crêpes

Creole Crêpes are delicious by themselves, or try them filled with Coconut Ice Cream (see page 109).

3 tablespoons melted butter

For the batter
2 cups all-purpose flour
pinch of salt
2 eggs
2 cups milk
⅔ cup coconut milk (see page 16)
2 tablespoons brandy or rum
2 tablespoons dark brown sugar
¼ cup melted butter
½ teaspoon ground cinnamon
⅛ teaspoon ground cloves
⅛ teaspoon grated nutmeg

For the sauce
⅓ cup brandy
⅓ cup granulated sugar
2 teaspoons ground cinnamon

Makes 12

1 Make the crêpe batter: Sift the flour and salt together into a large mixing bowl. Make a well in the center and gradually beat in the eggs, milk and coconut milk until the mixture forms a smooth batter.

2 Stir in the brandy, sugar, butter, cinnamon, cloves and nutmeg.

3 Heat an 8 inch skillet. Brush with a little melted butter and pour in about 2 tablespoons of the batter, enough to thinly coat the base of the pan. Tip the pan as you pour, so that the base is evenly coated.

4 Cook for 30 seconds then turn the crêpe over and cook for a further 30 seconds until golden brown. Remove with a spatula, roll up the crêpe and place in an ovenproof serving dish. Keep warm in a preheated very low oven while you cook the remaining crêpes.

5 Make the sauce: Put the brandy, sugar and cinnamon in a small saucepan. Place over low heat and cook for 2 minutes, until the sugar has melted. Remove from the heat, pour over the crêpes and serve immediately.

Rum and Banana Mousse

Bananas and rum are two ingredients which feature strongly in Caribbean cooking. And the two combine deliciously in this rich, alcoholic dessert.

2 tablespoons unflavored gelatin
¾ cup rum
3 ripe bananas, mashed
2 teaspoons vanilla
5 eggs, separated
pinch of salt
⅓ cup superfine sugar
2 cups heavy cream
⅛ teaspoon grated nutmeg

Serves 6

1 Sprinkle the gelatin over ¼ cup of the rum in a small ramekin or custard cup. Let soak for 5 minutes, then put the ramekin into a small saucepan of gently simmering water and heat gently for 2-3 minutes, until the gelatin has completely dissolved, stirring occasionally. Remove from the heat and let cool.

2 Put the bananas, the remaining rum and vanilla into a blender or food processor and work for 1 minute to a smooth purée. Set the banana mixture aside.

3 Using a hand-held electric mixer, beat the egg whites and a pinch of salt to stiff peaks. Gradually add half the sugar, beating constantly.

4 Beat the remaining sugar with the egg yolks until light and fluffy. Beat in 1¼ cups of the cream and continue beating for 5 minutes.

5 Add the banana mixture to the cream mixture, then fold in the egg whites and the dissolved gelatin.

6 Pour the mousse into a decorative glass bowl. Cover with plastic wrap and refrigerate for 2-3 hours or until set.

7 Beat the remaining cream in a bowl until firm. Remove the mousse from the refrigerator and pipe the cream on top in rosettes, sprinkle over the nutmeg and serve immediately.

Lime Meringue Pie

Lime Meringue Pie can be found in most of the Caribbean islands. A popular dessert, it is the perfect combination of sweet crisp meringue with tangy scented limes.

For the pastry
¾ cup all-purpose flour
pinch of salt
¼ teaspoon baking powder
2 teaspoons sugar
3 tablespoons butter

For the filling
¾ cup sugar
grated rind and juice of 5 limes
2 tablespoons all-purpose flour
4 tablespoons cornstarch
3 egg yolks

For the meringue
3 egg whites
pinch of salt
¾ cup superfine sugar

Serves 6

1 Make the pastry: Sift the flour, salt and baking powder into a mixing bowl. Add the sugar, then cut in the butter until the mixture resembles coarse meal. Using a knife, mix in 2 tablespoons of cold water until a stiff but non-sticky dough is formed. Knead lightly on a floured surface until smooth. Roll out and line an 8 inch pie dish. Chill in the refrigerator for 20 minutes.

2 Preheat the oven to 400°F. Fill the pie shell with waxed paper and pie weights and bake blind for 10-15 minutes or until it is lightly browned. Remove the paper and weights and let the pie shell cool.

3 Make the filling: Dissolve the sugar in 1¾ cups hot water in a medium saucepan over low heat. Add the lime rind and juice.

4 Mix the flour and cornstarch with 3 tablespoons of cold water in a small bowl to a smooth paste.

5 Stir the paste into the lime and sugar and bring to a boil over a medium heat, stirring constantly. Boil vigorously for 2 minutes then remove from the heat and let cool.

6 Add the egg yolks to the pan and place over a low heat. Bring the mixture to the simmering point, stirring constantly, but do not let it boil.

7 Remove from the heat and pour into the prepared pie shell. Let cool and set.

8 Preheat the oven to 350°F.

9 Make the meringue: Using an electric hand-held mixer, beat the egg whites and salt until firm. Add the sugar *very* gradually, beating mixture constantly until stiff peaks are formed.

10 Spread the mixture on top of the pie and bake in the center of the oven for 10-15 minutes or until the meringue is lightly browned.

11 Remove from the oven and serve hot or cold.

Lime Meringue Pie

Bananas Flambés

A simple dessert from Martinique which never fails to impress as it is brought still flaming to the table.

¼ cup butter, plus 1 tablespoon for greasing
6 large bananas
grated rind of ½ orange
juice of 1 orange
⅛ teaspoon grated nutmeg
¼ cup sugar
½ cup rum

Serves 6

1 Preheat the oven to 350°F. Grease a shallow ovenproof serving dish with the tablespoon of butter.

2 Put the unpeeled bananas on a small baking sheet and bake in the center of the oven for 10 minutes, turning once, until they have turned black.

3 Remove from the oven and when cool enough to handle, peel off the skins and arrange the bananas in the serving dish.

4 Preheat the broiler to high.

5 Mix the orange rind, orange juice and nutmeg together in a small bowl and pour over the bananas. Sprinkle over the sugar and dot surface with the remaining butter.

6 Place the bananas under the broiler for 6-8 minutes, or until the sugar is bubbling.

7 Meanwhile put the rum into a small saucepan and heat gently over low heat for 2 minutes.

8 Remove the bananas from the broiler. Ignite the rum in the saucepan with a match and pour the flaming rum over the bananas. Serve immediately while rum is still flaming.

Pink Grapefruit Bowl

In the Caribbean this dessert would be made with a sharp-tasting red-fleshed citrus fruit called shaddock or pomelo. The slightly sweeter grapefruit is believed to have developed from this fruit, which was first introduced to the Caribbean from Polynesia in the 17th century.

6 pink grapefruit
¼ cup rum
dash of Angostura bitters
1 cup superfine sugar

Serves 4-6

1 Thinly pare the rind from one of the grapefruit, using a fruit parer. Cut into matchsticks and reserve. Peel the grapefruits: Using a very sharp knife cut off a slice from both ends of each fruit. Then cut off the skin downward, taking the pith with it. Cut out each section from between the pithy membrane.

2 Put the sections into a large heatproof serving bowl. Pour in the rum and a dash of the bitters. Mix well together.

3 Melt the sugar in a heavy-bottomed saucepan over medium heat for 3-5 minutes until it is a caramel color, stirring constantly.

4 Off heat, pour over the grapefruit, leaving about 1 tablespoon of caramel in the pan.

5 Carefully pour ⅔ cup boiling water into the saucepan. Add the grapefruit matchsticks and bring to a boil over medium heat. Boil for 3 minutes. Drain and refresh under cold water.

6 Decorate the pink grapefruits with the blanched matchsticks and serve immediately.

Grapefruit Soufflé

Serve this creamy rich Grapefruit Soufflé as cold as possible, straight from the refrigerator.

¾ cup freshly squeezed pink grapefruit juice
1½ tablespoons unflavored gelatin
¾ cup superfine sugar
4 eggs, separated
2 tablespoons finely grated grapefruit rind
pinch of salt
1¼ cups heavy cream
½ cup crushed ratafia cookies

To decorate
⅔ cup heavy cream
8 ratafia cookies

Serves 6-8

1 Put the grapefruit juice into a small heatproof bowl. Sprinkle over the gelatin and let soak for 5 minutes. Stand the bowl in a small pan of gently simmering water for 1-2 minutes until the gelatin has completely dissolved, stirring occasionally. Remove from heat, and let cool for 5 minutes.

2 Put the superfine sugar, egg yolks and grapefruit rind into a heatproof mixing bowl. Place the bowl over a pan half-filled with simmering water and beat for 5 minutes with a hand-held electric mixer, until thick and creamy. Off heat, beat until cold.

3 Beat in the gelatin mixture. Cover and chill in the refrigerator for 15 minutes.

4 Using a hand-held electric mixer, beat the egg whites with a pinch of salt to stiff peaks. Beat the 1¼ cups cream in a separate bowl until firm, then fold into the egg whites.

5 Using a large metal spoon, gently fold the cream mixture into the grapefruit mixture. Pour half of the mixture into an 8-cup soufflé dish. Cover with the crushed cookies then gently spoon over the remaining mixture. Smooth the top with a knife and chill in the refrigerator for 3 hours, until set.

6 Whip the ⅔ cup cream until it holds its shape, then spread it over the top of the soufflé. Decorate with the whole ratafias and serve immediately.

Tropical Fruit Platter

This spectacular dessert speaks for itself. Tropical Fruit Platter can be made with any combination of tropical fruit arranged decoratively on a platter. The delicate passion fruit syrup allows the natural flavors of the other fruit to come through.

1lb watermelon, sliced, seeded and cut in wedges
1 small pineapple, halved, pared and cut in 2 inch slices, with the top reserved
1 papaya, peeled and sliced
2 mangoes, peeled and sliced
2 tangerines, peeled and sliced
2 bananas, sliced

For the syrup
pulp of 6 passion fruit
2 tablespoons sugar

Serves 6-8

1 Make the syrup: Put the passion fruit pulp, sugar and ½ cup water into a small saucepan. Bring to a boil over medium heat and boil vigorously for 1 minute. Off heat, strain the liquid through a fine mesh strainer into a pitcher, pushing the pulp with the back of a wooden spoon to extract all the juice. Let cool.

2 Place the pineapple top in the center of a large round glass serving dish. Arrange the fruit attractively in circles around it. Pour over the passion fruit syrup and serve immediately.

Pitch Lake Dessert Cake

This dessert cake is named after the Pitch Lake in Trinidad which provides the asphalt for constructing roads all over the world. Make it the night before and decorate with cream, chocolate and chocolate coffee beans just before serving. Use a vegetable parer to pare into curls.

¾lb individual dessert sponge shells or 1 small slab cake,
cut in squares
⅔ cup coffee liqueur
¼ cup milk
2 cups heavy cream

For the filling
8 squares (8oz) German chocolate, shredded
1 tablespoon instant coffee powder
5 eggs, separated
pinch of salt

To decorate
2 squares (2oz) German chocolate, pared in curls
chocolate coffee beans (optional)

Serves 6-8

1 Make the filling: Place the chocolate, coffee and 1 tablespoon of water in a heatproof bowl and place over a pan of simmering water. Cook for 5 minutes until the chocolate and coffee have melted.

2 Off heat, remove the bowl from the pan and let the mixture cool slightly. Beat in the egg yolks, one at a time.

3 Using a hand-held electric mixer, beat the egg whites with a pinch of salt to stiff peaks, then fold into the chocolate mixture with a metal spoon. Set aside.

4 Cut each of the sponge shells or squares in 3 slices lengthwise. Mix the coffee liqueur and the milk together in a bowl.

5 Line the base of an 8 inch loose-bottomed cake pan with waxed paper, then cover with a layer of the cake slices. Cut the pieces to fit, patchwork fashion. Sprinkle over one-third of the liqueur mixture, then cover with half of the mocha filling. Continue making layers in this way, ending with a layer of sponge and liqueur. Cover the top of the pan with plastic wrap and refrigerate overnight.

6 Run a knife around the inside edge of the cake pan, then unmold. Place a serving platter on top of the cake and invert the cake onto the platter. Remove the bottom of the pan and the waxed paper.

7 Whip the cream until firm then, using a slim spatula, completely cover the cake with the cream. Decorate the cake with chocolate curls and coffee beans, if using, and serve immediately.

Tropical Fruit Platter (front) and Pitch Lake Dessert Cake

Guava Ice Cream

Fresh guavas, which vary in color from white through to dark red, may be used for this delicious ice cream but canned guavas are equally suitable and often easier to obtain.

2 cans (16oz size) guavas, drained
6 eggs
¾ cup superfine sugar
2½ cups milk
1 teaspoon vanilla

Serves 6-8

1 Pureé the guavas in a blender or food processor. Strain the pulp to remove the seeds. Set the guava purée aside.

2 Lightly beat the eggs and sugar together in a medium-size heatproof bowl. Bring the milk to just below the boiling point, then pour into the egg mixture.

3 Place the bowl over a pan half-filled with simmering water. Cook, stirring constantly, for 30-35 minutes or until the custard is thick enough to coat the back of a spoon.

4 Off heat, stir in the vanilla and guava purée. Spoon the mixture into a china or glass dish. Let cool, then place in the freezer compartment for 2-3 hours or until the mixture is just beginning to freeze.

5 Remove from the freezer and beat well to break up the ice crystals. Return to the freezer for 3-4 hours, or overnight.

6 Remove from the freezer and place in the refrigerator 1 hour before serving, to allow the ice cream to soften slightly and ripen.

Coconut Ice Cream

This ice cream is found throughout the Caribbean in many different styles. This recipe uses evaporated milk, producing a sweet and rich ice cream slightly reminiscent of Indian kulfi.

grated flesh of 1 coconut
6 egg yolks
½ cup superfine sugar
2 cups evaporated milk
1 teaspoon vanilla

Serves 6-8

1 Make 2 cups coconut milk using the flesh of the coconut (see page 16).

2 Lightly beat the egg yolks and sugar together in a medium heatproof mixing bowl. Bring the evaporated milk to just below the boiling point, taking care not to let it burn. Then pour it into the egg mixture.

3 Place the bowl over a saucepan half-filled with simmering water. Cook, stirring constantly for 15-20 minutes, or until the custard is thick enough to coat the back of a spoon.

4 Off heat, stir in the vanilla and coconut milk. Spoon the mixture into a shallow china or glass dish and place in the freezer compartment and freeze for 2-3 hours or until it is just beginning to set.

5 Remove from the freezer and beat well to break up the ice crystals. Return to the freezer for 2 hours, beat again, then freeze for a further 1-2 hours.

6 Remove from the freezer and place in the refrigerator 1 hour before serving, to allow the ice cream to soften slightly and ripen.

Icebox Cake

Ice Box Cake is another specialty of the islands. The cake here will serve at least 12 and is best accompanied by strong black coffee.

½ cup butter
1 cup confectioners' sugar
1 egg, beaten
6 cups vanilla wafer crumbs
1½ cups dark rum

For the frosting
2 tablespoons butter
1 tablespoon rum
1 cup confectioners' sugar
2 tablespoons unsweetened cocoa

Serves 12

1 In a medium mixing bowl, cream the butter and sugar thoroughly together until the mixture becomes light and fluffy.

2 Add the beaten egg, vanilla wafer crumbs and rum and mix well.

3 Line a 9×5×2¾ inch loaf pan with waxed paper and press the mixture into the pan. Cover with plastic wrap and chill in the freezer for 1 hour.

4 Make the frosting: Melt the butter with the rum in a small saucepan over low heat. Add the confectioners' sugar, cocoa and 3 tablespoons warm water and stir with a wooden spoon until smooth and glossy. Off heat, cool to room temperature.

5 Remove the cake from the freezer and unmold on to a serving platter. Cover the top and sides with the frosting, using a slim spatula, and leave to set.

6 When the frosting has set, cover the cake with foil and return to the freezer for at least 2 hours.

7 To serve, cut the cake in thin slices and eat while still frozen.

CAKES, BREADS AND DUMPLINGS

The best fruit cakes in the world come from the Caribbean – they are rich, moist, full of fruit and rum, almost like puddings. They are often called Black Cakes because they are packed with dark rich dried fruit. Sizzling Fruit Cake (see page 112) is my own preferred lighter version of the Black Cake and is perfect to use as a Christmas or wedding cake. The Caribbean is also famous for its delicious sweet breads, such as coconut, banana and ginger, which always prove to be great favorites with children.

Chocolate Arrowroot Cake

Arrowroot is a powdery white starch made from the young rhizomes of the *Maranta arundinacea* plant grown on the island of St Vincent. It is used extensively in Caribbean cooking as a thickening agent and for making cakes, cookies and desserts.

½ cup butter, plus 1 tablespoon, for greasing
1½ cups all-purpose flour
½ cup arrowroot
½ cup unsweetened cocoa
1 cup superfine sugar
3 eggs
1 teaspoon baking soda
2 tablespoons instant coffee powder
½ cup milk
½ cup dairy sour cream
blanched tangerine peel, to decorate

For the topping
½ cup superfine sugar
¼ cup butter
4 squares (4oz) semisweet chocolate, broken in pieces

Makes an 8 inch cake

1 Preheat the oven to 325°F. Using 1 tablespoon of the butter grease an 8 inch round loose-bottomed cake pan.

2 Sift the flour, arrowroot and cocoa together in a bowl. Set aside.

3 Cream the butter and the sugar together in a large mixing bowl until the mixture is light and fluffy.

4 Add the eggs one at a time, beating well after each one.

5 Dissolve the baking soda and instant coffee in the milk and add to the egg mixture, alternately with the sifted flour mixture.

6 Add the sour cream and beat well. Pour the mixture into the prepared cake pan and bake in the center of the oven for 50-60 minutes, or until a skewer inserted into the center comes out clean.

7 Remove from the oven and let cool.

8 Make the topping: Put the sugar into a saucepan with 2 tablespoons of water and stir over medium heat until dissolved. Remove from the heat and whisk in the butter and chocolate until thick and smooth.

9 Remove the cake from the pan and spread the icing over the top. Cut the blanched tangerine peel into attractive shapes and use to decorate the cake.

Chocolate Arrowroot Cake

Sizzling Fruit Cake

Sizzling Fruit Cake acquired its name from the sound made when the rum is poured over the cake while it is still hot.

1¼ cups raisins
1¼ cups golden raisins
1¼ cups dried currants
1¼ cups candied cherries
1¼ cups pitted prunes
¼ cup chopped mixed candied peel
1½ cups dark rum
1 cup butter
1⅔ cups packed dark brown sugar
2 cups all-purpose flour
2 teaspoons baking powder
½ teaspoon ground cloves
1 teaspoon ground cinnamon
6 eggs
4 tablespoons molasses

Makes a 9 inch cake

1 Mix the raisins, dried currants, cherries, prunes and mixed peel together in a large bowl. Pour over 1¼ cups of the rum, cover with plastic wrap and set the fruit aside to soak for 24 hours, stirring occasionally.

2 Prepare a 10 inch round loose-bottomed cake pan, by lining first with brown paper then with waxed paper.

3 In a large bowl, cream the butter and sugar together until light and fluffy.

4 Sift the flour, baking powder, cloves and cinnamon together in another bowl.

5 Gradually add the flour mixture to the butter and sugar, alternating with the eggs, beating well after each addition.

6 Preheat the oven to 300°F.

7 Stir in the molasses, then fold the mixture into the soaked fruits. Mix well together until thoroughly combined.

8 Spoon the mixture into the cake pan and bake in the center of the oven for 2-2½ hours, or until a skewer inserted into the center comes out clean.

9 Remove the cake from the oven and gently prick it all over with a fork. Pour over the remaining rum and when it has stopped sizzling, cover and let cool in the pan.

10 Serve the cake sliced or, alternatively, keep it wrapped in a rum-soaked cloth then cover with a layer of marzipan and icing when required.

Banana Bread

Banana Bread is found throughout the Caribbean, each island having its own recipe. Some add golden raisins, others use Brazil nuts, and some include orange rind. This particular recipe was given to me by a friend from St Kitts.

2 tablespoons margarine, plus 1 tablespoon, for greasing
⅔ cup granulated sugar
¾ cup packed dark brown sugar
2 eggs, lightly beaten
3 cups all-purpose flour
1 teaspoon baking powder
1 teaspoon baking soda
½ teaspoon ground cinnamon
pinch of salt
3 large ripe bananas, mashed
⅓ cup milk mixed with 1 teaspoon lemon juice
1 teaspoon vanilla
⅔ cup pitted dates, chopped
1 cup walnuts, roughly chopped

Makes 2 loaves

1 Preheat the oven to 300°F.

2 Grease two 7×3 inch loaf pans with the 1 tablespoon of margarine.

3 Beat the remaining margarine with the white and brown sugars and eggs in a large bowl with a hand-held electric mixer until light and creamy.

4 Sift the flour, baking powder, soda, cinnamon and salt together in another bowl.

5 Gradually add the sifted flour mixture to the creamed mixture, beating thoroughly after each addition of flour.

6 Stir in the bananas, milk, vanilla, dates and walnuts.

7 Divide the mixture among the loaf pans and bake in the center of the oven for about 1 hour, or until a skewer inserted into the center of the loaves comes out clean.

8 Remove from the oven, run a knife around the inside of the pans and invert the loaves onto a wire rack to cool.

9 Serve spread with butter.

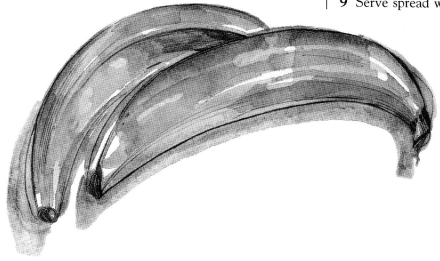

Gingerbread

A really spicy and gingery Gingerbread which can be eaten with or without butter. The longer it is kept the more moist it will become. If keeping, store in an airtight tin.

½ cup butter, plus 1 tablespoon, for greasing
2½ cups all-purpose flour
½ teaspoon salt
2 teaspoons baking powder
1 teaspoon baking soda
2 teaspoons ground ginger
¼ teaspoon grated nutmeg
½ cup molasses
⅔ cup packed dark brown sugar
¾-1 cup milk
2 eggs, beaten
1 teaspoon grated fresh gingerroot

Makes 1 loaf

1 Preheat the oven to 325°F. Lightly grease a 9×5×2¾ inch loaf pan with the tablespoon of butter.

2 Sift the flour, salt, baking powder, soda, ground ginger and nutmeg together into a large mixing bowl.

3 Melt the molasses, sugar and remaining butter in a small saucepan over low heat. Remove from the heat, let cool, then add the milk and eggs, mixing well.

4 Pour into the flour and mix together thoroughly. Fold in the grated ginger. Pour the batter into the loaf pan and cook for 50 minutes in the center of the oven, or until a skewer inserted into the center comes out clean.

5 Remove from the oven and let cool in the pan. Invert onto a platter and serve sliced, and spread with butter if wished.

Coconut Bread

Coconut Bread is very sweet and quite dry, almost a cake rather than a bread. It can be eaten with or without butter as preferred. Shredded coconut can be stored in a screw-top jar in the refrigerator for several weeks.

½ cup melted margarine, plus 1 tablespoon, for greasing
4 cups all-purpose flour
1 tablespoon baking powder
pinch of salt
2⅔ cups shredded coconut
¾ cup superfine sugar, plus 2 tablespoons, for glazing
⅔ cup raisins
1 egg, beaten
1¼ cups evaporated milk
1 teaspoon almond extract

Makes 2 loaves

1 Using the tablespoon of margarine, lightly grease two 7×3 inch loaf pans.

2 Preheat the oven to 350°F.

3 Mix the flour, baking powder, salt, coconut, ¾ cup sugar and the raisins together in a bowl.

4 Add the egg, evaporated milk, ½ cup margarine and almond extract and mix well together to a firm dough.

5 Divide the dough in half and fill the loaf pans. Mix the remaining sugar with 1 tablespoon of hot water and brush over the loaves.

6 Bake in the center of the oven for about 1 hour, or until a skewer inserted into the center of the loaves comes out clean.

7 Let cool in the pans, then remove and serve sliced, and buttered if wished.

Coconut Bread (front) and Gingerbread

Fried Yeast Rolls
Floats

Fried Yeast Rolls, or Floats as they are called in Trinidad, are the traditional accompaniment to a dish called accra, or salt fish cakes. Accra are similar to Stamp and Go (see page 25) but are made with the addition of yeast.

1 teaspoon sugar
1 teaspoon active dry yeast
3 cups all-purpose flour
1 teaspoon salt
¼ teaspoon cayenne
¼ cup shortening
⅓ cup oil

Makes 15

1 Dissolve the sugar in ¼ cup warm water. Sprinkle the yeast into the water and set aside for 10 minutes in a warm place.

2 Put the flour, salt and cayenne in a bowl. Cut in the shortening and rub it into the mixture with your fingertips until the mixture resembles fine meal.

3 Add the yeast and enough warm water, about ⅔ cup to make a soft dough. Knead the dough on a lightly floured surface until it is smooth and elastic. Return to the bowl, cover with a clean dish towel and leave in a warm place for 1½ hours, or until it has doubled in bulk.

4 Break off golf-ball size pieces and roll into balls, flouring your hands to prevent the dough sticking. Place on a baking sheet and leave to rise for another 20 minutes. Roll the risen balls out to about ¼ inch thick.

5 Heat the oil in a large heavy-bottomed skillet and cook, a few at a time, for 2-3 minutes, until cooked inside and golden brown on the outside.

6 Drain on paper towels and serve hot.

Cornmeal Dumplings

These popular if rather heavy dumplings are served with many of the more hearty dishes of the Caribbean islands.

1 cup all-purpose flour
¾ cup cornmeal
1 teaspoon baking powder
1 teaspoon salt
1 tablespoon minced fresh chives
3 tablespoons shortening

Makes 24

1 Put the flour, cornmeal, baking powder, salt and chives in a mixing bowl. Cut in the shortening and rub into the mixture with your fingertips until the mixture resembles coarse meal. Stir in ⅓ cup cold water to make a stiff dough. Roll the dough into balls to make dumplings.

2 Bring a large pan of salted water to a boil and drop in the dumplings. Cover the pan, lower the heat slightly and simmer vigorously for 10-15 minutes until dumplings are cooked.

3 Alternatively add the dumplings to a soup or stew and cook as above.

Cheese Corn Sticks
Surullitos

Cheese Corn Sticks, or Surullitos as they are called in Puerto Rico, make a good appetizer to pass around with drinks.

1 teaspoon salt
1½ cups cornmeal
1½ cups shredded Edam or Gouda cheese
1 teaspoon mild paprika
1 cup oil

Makes 28-30

1 Pour 3 cups water into a saucepan, add the salt and bring to a boil over medium heat.

2 Gradually pour the cornmeal into the boiling water, stirring constantly, and cook for 3 minutes until the mixture is thick and smooth.

3 Off heat, stir in the shredded cheese and paprika. When the mixture is cool enough to handle, roll into sticks measuring approximately 3×1 inches, wetting your hands from time to time to prevent the mixture from sticking.

4 Heat the oil in a skillet over medium heat. Cook the sticks a few at a time for 2-3 minutes until golden brown. Remove with a slotted spoon and drain on paper towels.

Fried Bread Rolls
Bakes

These Fried Bread Rolls are delicious served hot, split open and spread with butter or filled with Trinidad Fried Shark (see page 25).

Although they are best eaten as soon as they have been cooked, they can be cooked an hour before serving and kept warm in a low oven.

8 cups all-purpose flour
1 tablespoon salt
1½ tablespoons sugar
5 tablespoons baking powder
⅓ cup butter or margarine
oil, for deep-frying

Makes 20

1 Put the flour, salt, sugar and baking powder into a large mixing bowl.

2 Cut in the butter or margarine and rub into the flour with your fingertips until the mixture resembles coarse meal.

3 Gradually add about 2½ cups water, until the mixture forms a firm dough. Knead until smooth.

4 Divide into 20 pieces and roll each piece into a ball, using a little flour if necessary. Flatten with a floured rolling pin to about ¼ inch thick and 3 inches in diameter.

5 Heat ½ inch of oil in a deep skillet over medium heat. When the oil is hot, add the doughballs a few at a time. Lower the heat slightly and cook for 5-7 minutes, turning a few times, until golden brown, taking care not to burn them. Remove with a slotted spoon and drain on paper towels while cooking the remaining doughballs.

6 Place on a baking sheet and keep warm in a low oven until ready to serve.

DRINKS

Rum-based drinks are synonymous with the Caribbean. It is a liquor that is common to all the islands. There is light rum, golden rum and dark rum, each one with its own taste and character. White rum is ideal for mixing with mixers or fruit juices and for making popular cocktails such as Banana Daiquiri (see page 121). Golden rum is my own particular favorite for Rum Punch (see page 120) but it is also excellent for other rum-based drinks such as Cream Punch (see page 120). Dark rum has a heavy molasses flavor and is best used for cooking. And for those people who do not enjoy rum there are endless exotic and thirst-quenching fruit drinks to choose from.

Rum Punch

Every island in the Caribbean has its own version of Rum Punch. Most people follow the general rule of one sour, two sweet, three strong and four weak, though I tend to prefer another version – one sour, two sweet, three strong and no weak!

1 cup granulated sugar
½ cup fresh lime juice
1½ cups golden rum
1 cup crushed ice or ice cubes
dash of Angostura bitters
grated nutmeg

Makes about 3½ cups (Serves 4-6)

1 First make the sugar syrup: Put the sugar in a small saucepan. Pour in 1 cup cold water and bring to a boil over medium heat, stirring constantly. Lower the heat and simmer for 3-5 minutes, or until the sugar has dissolved and the liquid is clear. Remove from the heat and set aside until the sugar syrup has cooled.

2 When the syrup is completely cold, pour it into a large pitcher. Then add the lime juice, the golden rum and the ice or ice cubes and mix everything thoroughly together.

3 Pour into 4-6 wine glasses, add a dash of Angostura bitters and sprinkle over the nutmeg. Serve the rum punch immediately.

Cream Punch
Poncho de Crema

Cream Punch or Poncho de Crema is traditionally served at Christmas time in Trinidad. It is a very strong, rich egg nog, served over lots of crushed ice. It is guaranteed to create a festive mood!

1 egg, beaten
grated rind of ½ lime
1 cup condensed milk
¾ cup evaporated milk
1½ cups golden rum
1 cup crushed ice
dash of Angostura bitters
grated nutmeg

Makes about 4 cups (Serves 6-8)

1 Put the egg, lime rind, condensed milk, evaporated milk and rum into an electric blender and blend at high speed for 30 seconds.

2 Divide the ice between 6-8 wine glasses and pour over the cream punch. Add a dash of Angostura bitters and sprinkle over the nutmeg. Serve immediately.

On previous page, from the left: Rum Swizzle, Banana Daiquiri, Cream Punch, Bentley, Tropical Fruit Punch and Rum Punch.

Rum Swizzle

Rum Swizzle is a perfect combination for those who like their cocktails strong but not too sweet.

1¼ cups crushed ice
¾ cup white rum
juice of 2 limes
1 tablespoon superfine sugar
2 tablespoons orange-flavored liqueur

To decorate
2 lime slices
2 cocktail cherries

Makes 2 cocktails

1 Chill 2 cocktail glasses.

2 Put the crushed ice in a cocktail shaker. Pour in the rum, lime juice, sugar and orange-flavored liqueur. Shake well or swizzle.

3 Strain into the chilled cocktail glasses. Decorate with the lime slices and cherries and serve.

Bentley – The Teetotaller's Drink

It looks like a pink gin but is made with only lime juice, sugar, club soda and Angostura bitters – a favorite flavoring in many Caribbean drinks.

1¼ cups fresh lime juice
¼ cup superfine sugar
1¼ cups club soda
Angostura bitters

Makes about 2½ cups (Serves 4)

1 Chill 4 tall glasses.

2 Mix the lime juice with the sugar in a pitcher, stirring constantly until the sugar has dissolved.

3 Add ice cubes and pour in the club soda. Add Angostura bitters to taste, mix well together and serve in the chilled glasses.

Tropical Fruit Punch

This is a refreshing non-alcoholic drink, full of exotic and tantalizing tastes.

1 large ripe mango, puréed
1¼ cups pineapple juice
1¼ cups fresh orange juice
⅔ cup fresh lime juice
½ cup sugar syrup (see page 120)
crushed ice
4 teaspoons grenadine syrup
chopped pineapple, orange and banana,
to decorate (optional)

Makes about 2⅔ cups (Serves 4)

1 Put the mango purée, pineapple juice, orange juice, lime juice and sugar syrup in a large pitcher.

2 Add lots of crushed ice and mix well together with a long spoon. Pour into 4 wine glasses. Add a teaspoon of grenadine to each glass, decorate with the chopped fruit, if liked, and serve immediately.

Banana Daiquiri

When frozen Banana Daiquiri is like a banana sherbet – but the after-effects are quite different!

½ cup white rum
2 tablespoons superfine sugar
⅓ cup fresh lime juice
1 banana, sliced
2½ cups crushed ice
banana slices, to decorate

Makes 2 cocktails

1 Chill 2 cocktail glasses.

2 Put the rum, superfine sugar, lime juice, sliced banana and crushed ice into an electric blender and blend at high speed for 30 seconds.

3 Pour into the cocktail glasses and decorate with the banana slices. Serve immediately.

GLOSSARY

Ackee: The fruit of a West African tree brought to Jamaica in the 18th century by Captain Bligh. When ripe the pear-shaped scarlet pod bursts open, exposing the edible cream-colored aril. Canned ackee is available.

Banana Leaves: Used as a wrapping for certain dishes, giving the food a distinctive flavor. Available from some oriental markets and gourmet food stores.

Breadfruit: A large round green fruit with a bumpy thick skin. The creamy flesh can be roasted, baked, boiled or fried. Available both fresh and canned from West Indian markets.

Chayote: Also known as choco, christophene and cho-cho. A pear-shaped gourd, it has a delicate flavor and ranges in color from creamy white to dark green. Widely available fresh or canned from West Indian markets.

Dasheen: A tropical root vegetable, also known as eddoe, taro and "old cocoyam", like a large bark-covered round rutabaga. The leaves are used to make Callaloo. Available from West Indian markets.

Guava: Similar to a small quince in appearance with a green, yellow, pink or cream colored skin and an inner pulp full of small seeds. The ripe fruit can be eaten raw but more often it is made into a compote or "cheese" (compressed preserve). Widely available.

Hearts of Palm: The terminal buds of a variety of palm trees. These mild-flavored ivory-colored shoots are canned and exported throughout the world. Available from delicatessens and West Indian markets.

Mango: A tropical fruit much used in Caribbean cooking. The unripe fruit is used for making chutneys and relishes. When ripe the color may vary from green to bright red, with a sweet yellow juicy flesh encasing a large seed.

Molasses: A thick liquid residue derivative from sugar cane. Light molasses is used as a table syrup; dark molasses, which has a stronger flavor, is used in cooking.

Okra: Also known as okros, ladies fingers or bamie. A green, slightly hairy pod native to Africa, used to thicken soups, stews and also eaten as a vegetable. Widely available fresh, frozen and canned.

Papaya: A tropical fruit widely used in Caribbean cooking, similar in appearance to an elongated melon. Unripe, it is cooked as a vegetable or used to make relishes. Ripe, it is yellow or orange with a soft orange flesh filled with shiny gray or black seeds. It is then eaten raw like a melon with a squeeze of lime juice. Not to be confused with pawpaw, a native American fruit with a smoky flavor.

Peppers: It is the hot seasoning peppers that give Caribbean cooking its distinctive flavor. Care should be taken when handling them: do not touch your face or eyes after working with them and be sure to wash your hands thoroughly. They are available from West Indian markets. Chilies can be substituted but for a more authentic flavor add a dash of hot pepper sauce.

Pigeon Peas: Used in soups, stews or as a vegetable with rice. Available fresh, dried and canned from West Indian markets.

Plantain: Like a large banana but without the sweetness. It must be cooked before it is eaten. Sold in varying stages of ripeness from green to almost black. Widely available.

Salt Cod: Used in many of the traditional Caribbean dishes. Available on the bone or filleted and wrapped in plastic packages, from West Indian and some Italian markets.

Shaddock: The largest member of the citrus fruit family, introduced to the Caribbean from Polynesia. It has a thick rind and juicy bitter flesh, like a bitter grapefruit. It is thought the grapefruit evolved from the shaddock.

Sweet Potato: A starchy vegetable native to tropical America. The skin varies in color from brown to pink to white and the flesh also varies from orange to white. Extremely high in Vitamin C. Widely available.

Tannia: Also known as yautia or "new cocoyam". A starchy root vegetable similar to the dasheen. (see Dasheen).

Topi Tambo: A tropical root vegetable with a texture similar to water chestnut.

Yam: A tuberous root and one of the staple vegetables of the Caribbean. It comes in various shapes, with a bark-like skin and creamy yellow flesh which has a nutty flavor.

INDEX

A

Ackee:
  and Salt Fish 32
  and Cheese Soufflé 72
Africans 12
Amerindians 12
Anchovy and Orange Butter
  with Fish Steaks 40
Arrowroot Chocolate
  Cake 110
Arroz con Camarones 48
Avocado:
  Sauce, with Poached Fish 34
  Dip 32
  and Pink Grapefruit Salad
90

B

Bakes 117
Banana(s):
  Bread 113
  Daiquiri 121
  Flambés 104
  Green, Curried 81
  Green, Soused 90
  and Rum Mousse 101
  and Rice Stuffed Chicken 53
Barbecued:
  Chicken Wings 57
  Gingered barbecued
    Lamb 65
Bean Salad 88
Beef:
  Ground, Hash 62
  and Okra Stew 62
  Patties, Jamaican 33
Bread(s):
  Banana 113
  Ginger 114
  Coconut 114
  Fried Yeast Rolls 116
  Fried Bread Rolls 117
Breadfruit Oiled-down 76
Buljol 24

C

Cake(s):
  Chocolate Arrowroot 110
  Icebox 109
  Pitch Lake Dessert 106
  Sizzling Fruit 112

Callaloo 14
  Vegetable 72
Caribbean:
  Coleslaw 92
  Kabobs 58
Carrot and Raisin Salad 92
Cashews with Stuffed
  Pumpkin 70
Cassareep 12
Chayote Baked au Gratin 73
Cheese:
  Corn Sticks 117
  Shrimp-filled Edam
    Cheese 48
  Soufflé and Ackee 72
  Sauce, Plantains Baked
    in 74
Chicken:
  Barbecued Wings 57
  Banana and Rice Stuffed 53
  Consommé with Peppers 21
  in Coconuts 50
  Fricassee 53
  and Hearts of Palm Pie 52
  Pelau 54
  with Rice and Pigeon
    Peas 54
Chillies 11
Chocolate Arrowroot
  Cake 110
Chow Chow 96
Cilantro and Coconut with
  Fish 36
Cocido de Rinones 69
Coconut(s):
  and Black-Eyed Pea
    Soup 17
  Bread 114
  Chicken in 50
  and Cilantro with Fish 36
  and Cucumber Salad 93
  and Fish Soup 20
  Ice Cream 109
  and Mango Meringue 98
  Mold 100
  Sauce 77
Cod, Salt:
  Salad 24
  Fritters 25
  and Ackee 32
  Frizzled 36
Coleslaw, Caribbean 92
Coo Coo 85

Corn (meal):
  Cheese, Sticks 117
  Chowder 16
  Dumplings 116
  and Meat Packages 30
  and Okra Pudding 85
Court Bouillon de Poisson 37
Crab:
  Backs 45
  Gumbo (Okra) 46
  and Spinach Soup 14
  Stuffed 45
Crayfish and Rice Salad 44
Creole:
  cooking 13
  Crêpes 101
  Ratatouille 78
  Rice 81
Cucumber and Coconut
  Salad 93
Curried:
  Green Bananas 81
  Lamb with Lentils 66
  Shrimp and Pineapple 46

D

Desserts:
  Banana Flambés 104
  Coconut Ice Cream 109
  Coconut Mold 100
  Creole Crêpes 101
  Grapefruit Soufflé 105
  Guava Ice Cream 108
  Icebox Cake 109
  Lime Bombe and Mango
    Sauce 100
  Lime Meringue Pie 102
  Mango and Coconut
    Meringue 98
  Pink Grapefruit Bowl 104
  Pitch Lake Dessert Cake 106
  Rum and Banana
    Mousse 101
  Tropical Fruit Platter 105
Drink(s):
  Banana Daiquiri 121
  Bentley 121
  Cream Punch 120
  Rum Punch 120
  Tropical Fruit Punch 121
Dumplings, Cornmeal 116

E

Eddoes, Creamed 80
Egglant:
  in Coconut Sauce 77
  with Pork 58
Escovitch 24
Europeans 12

F

Fish 34-49
  and Coconut Soup 20
  with Cilantro and
    Coconut 36
  Fillets in a Lime Sauce 38
  Loaf 41
  Marinated Cooked 24
  Martinique Poached 37
  Mousse 22
  Pie 38
  Poached, with Avocado
    Sauce 34
  Salt, and Ackee 32
  Seafood Pancakes 49
  Steaks with Orange 40
Floats 116
Foo Foo 84
Flying Fish, Fried 40
Fruit:
  Tropical, Platter 105
  Tropical, Punch 121
Fritters:
  Black-Eyed Pea 84
  Salt Cod 25
  Tannia 74

G

Garlic and Pepper
  Sauce 97
Ginger(ed):
  Barbecued Lamb 65
  Bread 114
Goat Water 68
Grapefruit:
  Hot, and Orange Baskets 28
  Pink, and Avocado Salad 90
  Pink, Bowl 104
  Soufflé 105
Guava:
  Pork Chops 60
  Ice Cream 108

Gumbo (Okra):
  Beef 62
  Crab 46

H

Hearts of Palm:
  and Chicken Pie 52
  Salad 26

I

Ice Cream:
  Coconut, 109
  Guava, 108
Indians and Chinese 13

J

Jamaican Beef Patties 33
Jerusalem artichokes,
  Sautéed 77
Jug-Jug 12

K

Keshy Yena 12, 48
Kidney Stew 69

L

Lamb:
  Gingered Barbecued, 65
  Curried with Lentils 66
Lime:
  Bomb and Mango
    Sauce 100
  Meringue Pie 102
  Sauce 38

M

Mango:
  and Coconut Meringue 98
  Sauce 100
Martinique Poached Fish 37
Meat:
  Balls, Sweet and Sour, 64
  and Cornmeal Packages 30
  Salad, Mixed 69
Meringue:
  Mango and Coconut, 98
  Lime, Pie 102
Moros y Cristianos 78
Mousse:
  Fish 22
  Rum and Banana 101

O

Okra:
  and Beef 62

and Cornmeal Pudding 85
Purée and Spinach 72
in Spicy Tomato Sauce 82
Orange(s):
  and Anchovy Butter with
    Fish Steaks 40
  Hot, and Grapefruit Baskets
    28

P

Pancakes, Seafood 49
Pastelles 30
Papaya, Stuffed Baked 64
Pepper(s):
  with Chicken Consommé 21
  and Garlic Sauce 97
  Jelly 97
  Pot Soup 21
  and Rice Salad with Tomato
    Dressing 93
  Trinidad Sauce 95
  Wine 95
Pepperpot 12
Picadillo 62
Pickle, Spicy Mustard 96
Pie(s):
  Chicken and Hearts of
    Palm 52
  Corn 85
  Fish 38
  Lime Meringue 102
Pigs Feet, Soused 29
Pineapple:
  and Shrimp, Curried 46
  Spare Ribs 61
Piononos 68
Plantain(s):
  Baked in Cheese Sauce 74
  Balls 84
  Crisps 29
  Stuffed Rolled, 68
Poncho de crema 120
Pork:
  with Eggplant 58
  Caribbean Kabobs 58
  Chops, Jerked 61
  Chops, Guava 60
Pulses:
  Bean Salad 88
  Black Beans and Rice 78
  Black-Eyed Peas and
    Coconut Soup 17
  Black-Eyed Pea Fritters 84
  Curried Lamb with
    Lentils 66
Peas 'n' Rice 80
Pigeon peas and Rice,
  Chicken with, 54
Pumpkin:
  Soup 18
  Stuffed, with Cashews 70

Punch:
  Cream 120
  Rum 120
  Tropical Fruit 121

R

Raisin and Carrot Salad 92
Rice:
  and Banana Stuffed
    Chicken 53
  and Black Beans 78
  and Crayfish Salad 44
  Creole 81
  and Pepper Salad with
    Tomato Dressing 93
  'n' Peas 80
  and Pigeon Peas, Chicken
    with 54
  and Shrimp 48
Rum:
  and Banana Mousse 101
  Punch 120
  Swizzle 121

S

Salad(s):
  Avocado and Pink
    Grapefruit 90
  Bean 88
  Caribbean Coleslaw 92
  Carrot and Raisin 92
  Crayfish and Rice 44
  Cucumber and
    Coconut 93
  Hearts of Palm 26
  Rice and Pepper with
    Tomato Dressing 93
  Salt Cod, 24
  Sunshine, 88
  Tropical Spinach, 89
  Yam, 89
Salpicon 69
Sancoche 66
Sauces:
  Avocado 34
  Cheese 74
  Coconut 77
  Garlic and Pepper 97
  Lime 38
  Mango 100
  Spicy Tomato and
    Garlic 82
  Sweet Pepper 96
  Trinidad Pepper 95
Seasoning 11
Shark:
  Stewed, 42
  Trinidad Fried, 25
Shrimp:
  Curried, and Pineapple 46

-filled Edam Cheese 48
Pepper 45
and Rice 48
Watermelon
  Cocktail 26
Snapper, Red, Stuffed and
  Baked 42
Sopito 20
Soup(s): 14-21
  Black-Eyed Pea and
    Coconut 17
  Chicken Consommé with
    Peppers 21
  Corn Chowder 16
  Crab and Spinach 14
  Fish and Coconut 20
  Pepper Pot 21
  Pumpkin 18
  Tomato and Sweet Potato
    18
Souse 29
Spare Ribs, Pineapple 61
Spices 11
Spinach:
  and Crab Soup 14
  and Okra Purée 72
  Tropical, Salad 89
Stamp and Go 25
Stew(ed):
  Beef and Okra 62
  Goat Water 68
  Kidney, 69
  Plantation, 66
  Shark 42
Surullitos 117
Sweet Potato(s):
  Balls, Stuffed 82
  Candied, 76
  and Tomato Soup 18

T

Tannia Fritters 74
Tomato(s):
  Dressing 93
  Spicy, Okra in 82
  and Sweet Potato
    Soup 18
Topi Tambo, Sautéed 77
Trinidad Fried
  Shark 25
Turkey, Four-Stuffing
  Christmas 56

W

Watermelon and Shrimp
  Cocktail 26
Wine, Pepper 95

Y

Yam Salad 89